MAKING IT!

First published in the United Kingdom in 2014 by
Collins & Brown
10 Southcombe Street
London
W14 0RA

An imprint of Anova Books Company Ltd

For more information
on Mollie Makes
please visit
molliemakes.com

ISBN 978-1-90844-918-4

A CIP catalogue record for this book is available from the British Library.

10 9 8 7 6 5 4 3 2 1

Illustrations by Claudia Boldt

Reproduction by Mission, Hong Kong
Printed and bound by 1010 Printing International ltd, China

This book can be ordered direct from the publisher at www.anovabooks.com

Mollie
MAKES

MAKING IT!

Contents

Introduction

Whether it's making hand-knitted sweaters, sweet-smelling soaps using flowers and herbs from the garden, delicate silver jewellery or rustic pots and plates, there's something intrinsically satisfying about creating things with your own hands. Part of the pleasure comes from doing something that's so different to our normal working life: many of us spend a large part of our working day hunched over a computer or operating a factory machine, so crafting really gives us the chance to switch off from the daily grind and indulge our creative side. Another appeal of crafting is that, in this age of mass-produced goods, it's lovely to be able to surround yourself with beautiful objects that you simply can't find on the high street – designs that allow you to express your individuality and personal sense of style.

This book is aimed at people who want to take their crafting one step further and turn it from a hobby into a money-making operation. Different people will have different reasons for wanting to do this. Perhaps you want to earn some 'pin money', so that you can buy materials to do yet more crafting and make your hobby self-financing? Perhaps your home is bursting at the seams with all the things you've made and you desperately need to sell some of them in order to clear some space? Or perhaps you want to turn your crafting into a full-time business?

Whatever your reason, there are all kinds of things you can do to maximize your chances of success. This book takes you stage by stage through everything you need to know to set up a successful craft business, from researching your market and customers, developing your 'brand' and financing your business, to marketing and selling your creations. Sections on basic accounting and legal issues such as copyright and employment law will guide you through potential pitfalls; and there are tips throughout from some of Mollie Makes' favourite crafters to help you along the way.

There will be highs and lows; there will be times when you feel completely exhausted, both physically and mentally – but there will also be times when you have the thrill of hearing complete strangers compliment you on your work or seeing someone wearing your design. Above all, you will have the satisfaction of being your own boss and making money doing something that you love.

THE START OF SOMETHING BIG

I'm not sure I know of a crafter out there who hasn't pondered the possibility of turning their beloved hobby into their livelihood. The allure of doing your favourite things all day, whether it's the hands-on making, creative-thinking or simply being your own boss, is strong. Getting paid a decent wage to do what you love? Jackpot!

But as we all know, there's way more to it than that! And the reality of business can strike hesitation into even the most talented designer. There are some tough questions to answer, late nights to work, sacrifices to make and a lot to learn, and that's exactly what we hope to guide you through in this book. With tips from a collection of our savvy friends in the craft industry, there's plenty of inspiration along with large doses of reality. Do share your journey with us on social media – you can find us at @molliemakes on Twitter and Instagram, and at www.facebook.com/molliemakes.

This could be the start of something big – you can do it!

Lara

Lara Watson
Editor, Mollie Makes

Chapter 1

First steps

Do your research

So – you're passionate about crafting, your family and friends seem to love what you create, and you think you can earn some money from it. Where do you go from here?

Unfortunately, no matter how much you enjoy making things and no matter how gorgeous they look, that's no guarantee that you'll be able to make a successful business out of it. The first thing you need to do is research your market. And that means finding out not only **what** sells, but **who** you can sell it to and **where** you can sell it.

You don't need a qualification or experience in sales and marketing to do this – but you do have to put yourself out there and find out if enough people are actually prepared to hand over their hard-earned cash to make your business profitable. So before you start ordering truckloads of fabric, beads or whatever other raw materials you use, canvass opinion from as many people as you can to find out what they really think about your work.

If you're used to beavering away in your spare bedroom or workshop day after day, with only the cat for company, this can come as quite a shock to the system! There's no doubt that some people find it easier to talk to potential customers than others, but if you're going to succeed in business – any business – you'll need to get over such inhibitions pretty quickly.

Family, friends and work colleagues are a good starting point – but bear in mind that you may not get a totally honest opinion, as they won't want to upset or offend you. The chances are, not only do you go to craft markets regularly, but you are also already selling your work at local craft markets or fairs and have several products in your range; make a note of which ones sell and which ones don't and try to work out why. And instead of second guessing, talk to your customers and find out what they like and don't like. Craft fairs are generally very relaxed, friendly places and most people will be only too happy to chat. If another seller is in direct competition with you, ask your customers what made them choose your product. Do they think your product is good value? If they were looking for a similar product on the Internet, what search terms would they use on Google?

Look at the competition, too. Are other people selling similar things? If so, can you amend your designs to make them more individual, so that they really stand out? How does your competitors' packaging and pricing compare with yours? What 'message' comes across about their product? Without directly copying their ideas, visit their market stall and check out their websites and Facebook pages to see if there are any lessons that you can apply to your own business. You can also use your own blog and Facebook page to conduct mini surveys and find out how potential customers react to your work (see page 80).

See also:
Find your USP, page 13
Costs and pricing, page 56

RESEARCH YOUR CUSTOMER

The key thing is to put yourself in your customer's shoes. Too often, craftspeople are so caught up in designing and making their product that they forget that it is the customer's wants, not their own, that they must satisfy.

Knowing who your potential customers are, what they want and what motivates them to buy is every bit as important as knowing how to create your designs, if not more so. You also need to build up a profile of your typical customer.

Try to find answers to the following questions:

> Are your customers mostly male or female? What age group and social demographic do they fall into? Knowing the answers to these questions will not only help you develop your product range, but it will also help when you're designing packaging and marketing material.

> Do your customers think your product is correctly priced? Would they be prepared to pay more?

> What are your customers' main reasons for buying that particular product? For example, is it to make them look or feel good? To keep up with current fashions? To support the local economy and encourage sustainable business? You need to give them a reason for buying that your competitors can't match. (See Find your USP, opposite.)

> Are they buying the item for themselves or for someone else? Remember that the person who buys your product may not be the end user, so it's the buyers you need to appeal to. If you make kids' clothes, for example, toddlers love brightly coloured clothes with fun motifs, but they won't care what fabric or yarn they're made from, while busy mums will want to be sure the item is machine washable – and it's the mums who are buying!

> Where do your customers normally buy similar products – for example, in a shop or online? This may help you work out where best to sell your work.

> Where do your customers find out about products similar to yours – by word of mouth? From magazines or newspapers (and if so, which ones)? From radio adverts? Knowing this can help you to target your marketing more effectively further down the line.

FIND YOUR USP

In order for your product or product range to appeal to customers, you need to give it a USP.

The term 'USP' stands for Unique Selling Proposition. That sounds like a piece of marketing jargon, but it's a useful shorthand way of reminding yourself that you need to focus at every stage – production, sales and marketing – on what makes your product special. Unless you can pinpoint this, you cannot target your sales efforts successfully.

Your USP is what makes your business stand out; it's what makes you different and gives you a special place in the minds of your potential customers. With a huge range of products out there, you have to answer the question, 'Why should I buy from you?'.

The price of a product is undoubtedly a factor in whether or not people buy it – but price is never the only reason people buy something. Obviously you want to achieve the best price you can, but you don't want to price yourself out of the market.

In a craft business, a large part of your USP might be the fact that your product is handmade: everyone expects to pay more for something that is produced by hand than for something that is mass produced. The quality of the craftsmanship is also something that you can emphasize and that people would expect (and be willing) to pay a premium for; if you have qualifications or experience in a relevant skill, let customers know what it is. For example, you could mention that you studied fashion and textile design at college, or have several years' experience as a professional silversmith.

As well as your skills, if you are running a small business, sometimes your personality can make a difference. If you have a personality that resonates with others then you can create something that no one else can compete with directly.

Or maybe it's the things you use to create your product that make it special. If your soaps and bath products are completely organic, or you source your fabric from a weaving cooperative high in the Andes, or your felt is made from 100% merino wool, make sure you say so. Things like this differentiate your work from that of other people and give it an added perceived value.

Sustainability and environmental issues such as food miles are another aspect you can emphasize. Perhaps you're using natural materials such as driftwood or shells, or recycled fabrics? Are you making furniture from old railway sleepers or soft furnishings from recycled clothing?

Maybe your product could be customized or personalized in some way – by appliquéing a child's name onto your handmade baby bibs, for example.

Once you have pinpointed your USP you need to communicate it clearly and often. This is where branding and design come in: a great name, well-designed branding (see page 16) and beautiful packaging can really help with promotion of a product, and along with a clear message can really tie the idea of your unique concept together. And don't assume people will remember your USP: you also need to be prepared to let people know on a regular basis why your business is different.

Finally, there are more intangible aspects to consider – friendly service, reliable after-sales service, swift delivery and so on – all of which play a part in whether or not a customer is likely to return to you.

TRY FOR YOURSELF

1) Devise a short questionnaire to find out what potential customers think about your work and help you build up a customer profile. To encourage people to fill it in, you could give away a prize to one respondent.

2) To really focus your mind on your USP, see if you could write it as a 'tweet' of no more than 140 characters. For example:

'We make one-off statement pieces of jewellery from recycled vintage pieces for fashion-conscious women in their 20s and 30s.'

'Miniature Crochet Animals - Sweet and Precious Gifts for Everyone – Teeny tiny and adorable animals and their cute friends are looking for a new home.'

'Vintage inspired dresses. We create original designs that we stock along with carefully curated boutique finds.'

You might have to exceed 140 characters, but it's a useful exercise!

WHAT NEXT?

Once you've gone through this process, you need to take the next – and most difficult – step: you need to set aside any preconceived ideas you might have had about your product and be brutally honest with yourself. What sets your business or product range apart from all the others? How can you use your USP to make customers want to buy from you? Do you really have the makings of a successful business?

If the answer to that last question is a resounding 'no', don't be too despondent. It's hard to give up a dream – but when you're starting a business, your dreams have to be rooted in reality. Try to see even lukewarm responses to your ideas as a positive rather than a negative: at least you've found out before you spend a lot of time and money developing something that won't pay off. Instead, use what you've learned to adapt or change your business idea and meet the problem head on.

If the answer is 'yes', then you're in a strong position to move on to the next stage – developing your 'brand'.

Building your 'brand'

Put simply, your 'brand' is the personality of your business — it's how it appears to others, how it sounds, looks and feels. Once it's created, you'll need to work hard to preserve it.

WHAT'S IN A NAME?

This is one of the most important decisions you have to make, as it sets the tone for your business. It sums up who you are and what you do.

Start by jotting down any keywords that seem relevant to your product and USP. Your list might include words like vintage, recyclable, personalized, luxury, practical, your own name, your location... Try out every combination you can think of, and ask family and friends for their input, too. What word(s) can you use in your name that reflect your USP and business ethos?

It's important to choose something that people can remember easily. You also need to ask yourself if it is Internet-friendly. With so many sales being made online these days, you need something that's easy to find (and spell!), but not so common that there are thousands of businesses out there with similar names. For example, if your surname is Smith, then 'Smith's Crafts' would probably turn up hundreds of similar names on a search engine such as Google.

Beware of being too specific, however, as you do not know how your business may evolve in the future. For example, at the moment your business may revolve around making personalized patchwork quilts and wall hangings — but if you call it something like 'Quilts to Order' and branch out at a later date into making items like quilted cushions or bags, your business name will not reflect that. Customers looking for quilted cushions and bags will not easily be able to find you.

Once you think you've got a name, do a thorough Internet search to see if anyone else is using that name or one very similar to it. Start by checking the kind of areas in which you'll be trading initially: are any other crafters on Etsy or Not on the High Street trading under a name similar to yours?

In the UK, check with Companies House (www.companieshouse.gov.uk) to see if any businesses are actually registered under that name. You will also need to find out if your chosen name is available for Internet use (see page 24); these should usually go hand in hand. In the USA the US Small Business Adminstration (www.sba.gov) provides advice on choosing business names.

DEVELOPING A LOGO

A logo can take many forms. It can be a graphic symbol (Apple), the initials of the company name (gsk – GlaxoSmithKline), a combination of the company name and a graphic symbol (Rowan Yarns), a name of an individual designed to look like a hand-written signature (Cath Kidston) or any number of other permutations.

What do you want your logo to communicate? Start by listing the keywords that best describe your business – then think about how you might portray those qualities visually. If you're making really funky steampunk jewellery, for example, then a classic italic typeface might not be your best choice. For organic soaps and scents, you might turn to white or pastel colours, an elegant style of type and images that evoke the purity of the natural world; for knitted toys, you would probably look at much brighter colours, a modern typeface and maybe even a cartoon-style character to reflect the age of your end users.

RESTRICTIONS ON BUSINESS NAMES

> The Companies Act 2006 sets out the restrictions and requirements in relation to business names. A 'business name' is any name under which a person carries on business other than their own.
> There is no requirement to register business names, but there are a number of restrictions and formalities that need to be adhered to.
> Detailed information on business names and company names can be found on the Companies House website, which oversees the Register of Companies in the UK and provides information on many aspects of company law (www.companieshouse.gov.uk).

Examine brands you like and brands you don't. Who do they appeal to and why? Which have the most resonance with your own brand? Looking at other companies' logos will help you to formulate your own ideas.

Sketch out your ideas, no matter how rough. Remember that your logo will need to look good at all sizes, from business cards and bags to shop windows. Make sure it works in both colour and black and white: it may end up being reproduced in black and white in a newspaper.

If your budget allows, consider hiring a branding agency or graphic designer to help you create an identity. If your budget won't quite stretch to that, why not enquire at a local university to see if any design students are looking to work on a branding project? Not only will this help to keep costs down but it will also provide the student with material for their portfolio. Alternatively, attend an evening class to allow you to get to grips with computer packages such as Illustrator and Photoshop.

Whichever route you choose, spend time investigating the options. And trust your instincts: if you like the look and feel of your branding, chances are you'll attract exactly the type of customers you had in mind.

TRY FOR YOURSELF

Draw up a list of a dozen or so established companies and ask yourself what images their names conjure up. Is it a family-run business that prides itself on exceptional service to its customers? Is it an individual designer whose name is a byword for a particular style? Does it bring to mind a specific product? Does it embody a particular USP, such as value for money, an emphasis on natural ingredients, a specialist skill? Now apply the same analytical thought process to a shortlist of names for your own business. What image do they conjure up?

A good logo is distinctive, appropriate, practical, graphic, simple in form and conveys an intended message. The 'Mollie Makes' logo ticks all of these boxes to complement our company ethos: 'living and loving handmade'.

FINDING THE RIGHT HELP

If you're thinking of commissioning someone to help you, it's important to find the right person for you – someone who understands and can communicate your vision. Expect to be challenged but don't be tempted to commit to something you're not entirely sure about.

Once your brand has been created, your designer or agency should give you a document entitled 'brand guidelines' or something similar. A brand guideline document is important as it explains what a brand stands for, how it is expressed, and how the creative elements fit together in all communications. Typically, it will contain information about the fonts used in your branding and the size they should be used at, and which colours should be used – some guidelines may even interpret what specific colours represent. The idea is that consistency across all areas of your brand will encourage trust among your customers. Keep this document safe, as you will need to refer to it often when working on new materials such as leaflets and business cards.

FIND OUT MORE

> Contact UK-based Business Link (www.gov.uk) for advice on branding.
> The Crafts Council of Ireland (www.ccoi.ie) offers training and courses.
> Wherever you are in the world you can benefit from the advice of the Design Council (www.designcouncil.org.uk) and their downloadable free Power of Branding resource.
> If you're looking to access designers from around the world, then CrowdSPRING (www.crowdspring.com) might just be the answer. Tell them what your project is and allow designers to come to you.

See also:
Setting up your website, page 24
Creating effective marketing material, page 86

Looking at logos

{ *Encapsulating everything you want to say about your business may sound daunting, but this is the fun part! These companies have all created successful branding.*

JANE FOSTER DESIGNS (www.janefoster.co.uk)
> As an artist herself, Jane Foster was able to create her own branding. She has used her own distinctive appearance as the basis of the logo.
> In addition to the Jane Foster 'character', the use of the signature makes this company seem friendly, approachable and gives customers a personal link with Jane.
> The design is very bold and simple, like Jane's work. Its simplicity means that it is a flexible logo that can be used in different ways.
> For more about Jane Foster, see page 84.

THE DESIGN TRUST (www.thedesigntrust.co.uk)
> The Design Trust is an online business school for designers and makers, and helps creative professionals to start and run their own craft or design business.
> This simple but striking logo resembles the tabs of an organizer file or website. The design is friendly and business-like, skillfully reflecting the school's expertise in developing the organizational skills of up-and-coming creatives.
> For more about The Design Trust, see page 146.

WHAT DELILAH DID (www.whatdelilahdid.com)
*> What Delilah Did designer Sophie Simpson
describes her work as an 'amalgamation of antique
heirloom embroidery and modern design'. The
traditional feel of her branding takes its inspiration
directly from Sophie's work.*
*> This logo was created for What Delilah Did
by illustrator Julianna Swaney. They worked together
on the design to create a simple logo that suits the
company's ethos.*
*> The website address is included as well as the
company name.*
> For more about What Delilah Did, see page 62.

GILLIANGLADRAG (www.gilliangladrag.co.uk)
*> This logo makes use of bright colours and
geometric patterns to conjure up the fun, carnival-
like atmosphere of Gillian's branding, and also her
shop, The Fluff-a-torium.*
*> Gillian has a background in graphic design, so she
is very involved in all her branding.*
*> The name of the company is very prominent
across the centre of the design. This logo is used on
the packaging for Gillian's kits, as well as her website
and shop – unifying every strand of her business.*
> For more about Gilliangladrag, see page 76.

Expert advice from...

Claire Hartley, graphic designer

Claire Hartley (www.clairehartley.com) specializes in branding for start-ups and small companies to help them create or develop their visual identity. She recently worked with tableware designer Fenella Smith (www.fenellasmith.com). We caught up with Claire to find out what it's like to work with makers.

MM: What does the process involve?
CH: It covers everything from tone of voice, a logo marque, typography, colour and imagery. Producing brand guidelines is a great way to bring all the design together and ensures that the brand is consistent across all media, whether it is printed literature, stationery, exhibition material or packaging.

MM: Do you enjoy working with other creatives?
CH: Working with other designers is really interesting and it's a lovely opportunity to learn about another craft, too. Being creative really helps, especially at the brainstorming stage.

MM: How did you come to work with Fenella Smith?
CH: Fenella found my site while searching for illustrative designers and got in touch. We met in Henley-on-Thames and I knew immediately she'd be a really good client. Fenella felt her brand books needed a new approach, reflecting the handmade attributes and reinforcing the products' British credentials. Once I had a good understanding of her business, I produced mood boards and presented my ideas. The process is important to me and I like to ensure the client is involved throughout from initial brainstorming to first iterations and final sign-off. I've now produced two brand books for Fenella, plus some packaging.

MM: Do you think makers are nervous about the expense of seeking professional help?

CH: I think people do worry, yes. But that's why choosing who to work with is so important. Good process is integral to a project, as is trust. Being designers, we are all very precious of our work and the thought of somebody else interpreting that wrongly – and charging you for it, too – can be daunting. I'd advise working with small agencies or individuals so you'll be speaking directly to the designer (rather than through an account manager) and prices will be much more reasonable. I have a home studio so my day rate is less than half that of an agency, because my overheads are lower.

MM: What elements go into creating a strong brand?

CH: For me, tone of voice is really important. Whether you're an individual maker or a small company, all communication needs to feel like it's coming from the same person / people. It's essentially your brand's personality and what makes it distinct from its competitors, covering everything from the language used in emails to the visuals used in marketing. A good place to start is to look at your brand's values.

MM: What advice would you give to makers starting a new business?

CH: Being a sole trader myself and working from home, I think I'd say social media is one of the most powerful assets to have! I believe in the old saying 'it's not what you know, it's who you know' and you'll be surprised by how many queries I've had answered or doubts that have been restored by fellow creatives online. Word of mouth is a powerful tool, so it's a great (and free) way to get your products out there.

{ Top tips }

Claire on working with a designer

> Pick up the phone or meet your designer face to face – a conversation will give you a great insight into a designer's process and help you to share thoughts and ideas in a spontaneous way.

> Think carefully about your brief and try to include everything you would like the brand identity to achieve – the more a designer has to work with the better.

> If you're not entirely clear what you want, be open to suggestions – that's what professionals are there for. You might be pleasantly surprised by a new approach.

> Don't be wary of asking for costs, either, as we're used to quoting and won't be offended if you don't use us in the end.

Setting up your website

These days, no business can survive without its own website. From marketing to selling your work, the Internet is key – even if you're still in the early stages and not yet ready to go full time with your crafting business. Fortunately, setting up a website is nowhere near as difficult as you might think.

REGISTERING YOUR DOMAIN NAME

The first thing you need to do is decide on and register your domain name. This is your website's 'address'. Make sure it's easy to remember, reasonably short, and easy to spell. It's not expensive to register and you retain ownership of that domain name for as long as you pay for and renew it. (If you fail to renew and let it lapse, even for a day or two, someone else could buy it – so make sure you don't let that happen!)

If your chosen domain name is available, register it quickly. It's also worth registering variations (.com, .net and so on) in case someone else comes along and takes that name, as that could cause confusion for your customers – particularly if you're both selling similar products.

The fact that a domain name isn't available does not necessarily mean that someone is already using it for their own business: there are companies who buy up domain names in the hope that it's someone else's ideal name and they will offer to buy it from them.

In order to search to see whether a domain name has been registered it is necessary to carry out a WHOIS search. A WHOIS search is an online search facility that provides details of domain name registrations. Many hosting companies and registrars (such as Nominet in the UK) provide WHOIS search facilities and these are free to use.

There are different types of domain name extensions, for example: .com (a top-level domain name); .co.uk, .me.uk, .biz (second-level domain names); or the name itself. In some cases, top-level domain names have been registered, but other extensions remain available.

Web-hosting companies (see below) will generally do domain registration for you.

CHOOSING A WEB HOST

The next thing you need to do is choose a 'web host' – a company that has many computers connected to the Internet. When you put your web pages on their computers, everyone can connect to and view them.

Some web hosts are free – but the downside of this is that, because the web hosts have to make money somehow, most of them impose advertising on your website. Most web hosts charge a monthly, quarterly or annual fee. Make sure you know what you're getting for your money – but as your website will be such an important part of your business, price should not be the only factor in your decision.

With so much choice available, it can be hard to know which web host to go for. Decide which features are important to you (see page 26), check out comparison websites and consumer reports, and talk to friends and other crafters to see which ones they recommend before you sign on the dotted line. There are several things that you need to consider when choosing a web host.

Reliability and speed of access

Not only should the web host be fast, it should also guarantee its uptime (the time when it is functional). Look for a minimum uptime of 99%.

Data transfer, or bandwidth

This is the amount of bytes transferred from your site to visitors when they browse your site. Generally, 3 GB traffic per month is adequate for a simple site. Check what your monthly limit is, otherwise you may find yourself faced with a hefty bill. Text consumes very little bandwidth. Pictures use more but can be minimized by compressing photos. Luckily, due to the limitations of display technology, you can shrink photos a lot without affecting the picture's look. Pictures in the range of a few tens of kB size are usually perfectly acceptable for most illustrations. Videos make huge demands on bandwidth, far too much for normal websites, so most people host these on specialist sites such as YouTube and then use a link to access them. Bandwidth is also controlled by how many visitors you get. If your site becomes popular you'll need to increase it.

Disk space

This is the amount of space you have available for your website. If you don't have music or videos, you will probably need a relatively small amount of space, so even if your host is offering a whopping 100 GB, you may not need it.

Technical support

Can you get support 7 days a week, 24 hours a day? Things tend to go wrong at the most inconvenient times and you don't want to lose business by being offline at weekends or on bank holidays.

Email addresses and mail forwarding

Can you set up whatever email addresses you want on your domain, so that mail can be forwarded to your current email address, or placed in a mail box on your web-hosting account itself?

SSL (Secure Server)

If you are planning to sell goods through your website, check whether the web host allows you to set up SSL. Naturally, this involves additional charges. You will definitely need SSL if you are going to collect credit card payments yourself (see page 142); if you're using a company such as PayPal, which collects credit card payments on your behalf, you won't need it. If you use SSL, it is important to put all customer information through secure pages – not just the final credit card details. Otherwise some customers may refuse to use your site if they think that their personal details may be transmitted over the web unencrypted.

DESIGNING YOUR WEBSITE

Unless you're a technical wizard, it's unlikely that you'll actually be designing and putting your website pages together yourself. Fortunately, you don't have to.

One option, if you can afford it, is to hire a professional web designer to do the job for you. Take the time to make sure they're the right person for the job: you need to be sure not only of their technical expertise, but also that they'll deliver the right 'look' for your business.

TRY FOR YOURSELF

As with branding, you can learn a lot about what to include on your website (and what to avoid!) by looking at what other people have done. Make a note of features that you like on other crafters' websites – what they put in their blog, how they set out any gallery pages, how they describe their products – and decide how you want to deal with these features on yours.

Another option is to use a web host's template service (for example, www.1and1.co.uk), which allows you to slot your text and images into a ready-made template with a choice of layouts, themes, fonts and background colours. Most offer several subscription packages, depending on the facilities that you want, along with a free 'try-before-you-buy' period of 14 or even 30 days.

MAKING YOUR WEBSITE ACCESSIBLE AND USER-FRIENDLY

Remember that your website is not just an online photo album to show how pretty your creations are – although that obviously plays a part. Its main purpose is to encourage people to buy your work. Make sure your customers can navigate quickly and easily around the site and find the information they need. In short, put yourself in your customer's shoes.

Imagine, for example, that you've just opened a page about accessories such as bags, gloves and scarves. Initially, you don't want to read reams of text about each one – you just want to get a broad idea of the range on offer. So have a one-line description on the first page, then a more detailed description on another page when your customer has clicked on the item he or she is interested in.

When they get to the detailed description, ask yourself what they need to know. In a real shop, they can pick up the item, feel it, and see how big it is. Online, you have to provide them with that information. So if you're selling vintage fabric pieces, for example, is it dress cotton weight or upholstery weight? What's the total size and how big is the pattern repeat? If you're selling jewellery, are your earrings 2.5 cm (1 in) or 5 cm (2 in) long and how heavy are they? (If they've been photographed on a plain background, no one will have any idea of the scale.) Is the price and any post and packing charge clear? Can they move easily from this page to the checkout?

Make sure the links from the first page to the product description work quickly and effectively; if people have to wait for a page to download, they're likely to lose interest – and when that happens, you've lost a customer.

If you're using a navigation bar or panel, make sure it's in the same place on every page, so that visitors don't have to hunt for it every time.

In addition to your navigation bar, provide shortcuts to places visitors are likely to want to go to – for example, from 'Products' to 'Buy'. Don't force your visitors to have to go back to your main page every time they need to visit another page.

Expert advice from...

Daniel Phillips, online marketing expert for Sorbet Design

Sorbet Design (www.sorbetdesign.co.uk) offers website and print design services for independent craft businesses and can help small businesses to generate more hits and, in turn, more customers. Here, Daniel shares with us his tips for good website development.

FIVE TIPS FOR USING PHOTOGRAPHS ON YOUR WEBSITE

1. Make sure the photos are crisp and not fuzzy or out of focus: take care with your photography and edit your photos carefully – only the best will do.
2. Make sure images are scaled correctly: products will look odd if the height and width are not in proportion.
3. Shrink photos to the actual size they will be on the web page: for example, 300 x 150 pixels. This will look crisper compared to altering photo sizes in web design software. This will also help to compress the file to a sensible size (see bandwidth, page 25).
4. Crop images to focus on what's important: your product should be the star of the picture.
5. Try different shapes: vary the size and shape of your images to give visual interest to the pages.

MM: What should be included on a website?

DP: Make sure your site has good content about what you do, what you sell, and what makes you different. Make sure you constantly add new content (maybe write a blog about your business or day-to-day activities) and make sure you shout about this on social networking sites such as Facebook and Twitter.

MM: How should a website be ordered?

DP: The titles on all of your web pages need to be relevant to the content on that page. Each page of your site should be unique and your titles should reflect this. They are the most important single factor in terms of on-page Search Engine Optimization (SEO). Get them right and you already have an advantage over your competitors. Your descriptions for each page should also be unique. They won't help you rank higher in the search results, but they are used by Google in the search results and a good and relevant description can encourage people to click through to your site rather than to another in the results.

MM: Should makers think more like their customers?

DP: Yes. All too often, people write content on their site from their point of view. You need to constantly be thinking about what your customers want to read, and write for them. This is particularly true when writing content to help you rank for particular search phrases in Google. Don't try and rank for the keyword phrases you use for your products, but instead think of what your customer will be searching for – and use those terms and phrases.

{ *Top tips* }

Daniel on effective websites

> Make sure your site includes your phone number and a contact form that is simple to use, so that customers can contact you at any time. Including your address details can help you to rank for regional searches, too.

> Find your niche, and then think of the keyword phrases that match your niche: if you make cushions, always refer to them as handmade or hand-embellished when describing them.

> Use social networking sites to help drive traffic to your site and help stimulate a buzz around your business. Be yourself and be professional. Show your human side, as this will endear you to your customers – but don't moan.

> Giving away products as prizes might sound like a way to burn money, but it can be a great way of stimulating sales. Again, create a buzz about your competitions and encourage others to talk about them and share them on Facebook and Twitter.

> It's easy to look at updating your website as a chore that you'll get round to eventually. But it's a good idea to dedicate 20 minutes or so every day to adding or updating the content on your site and promoting your site and your business on Facebook and Twitter. If you keep on top of it, you might even enjoy it!

Mollie Makes talks to...

Spinster's Emporium

Donna Bramhall founded Spinster's Emporium (www.spinstersemporium.co.uk), which sells DIY craft kits and vintage fabric, after becoming frustrated with the lack of choice in fabric for fashion students. The company is now run by Stephanie Weston Smith and Donna has moved on to a new creative business called Haberdasher Me. The Spinster's Emporium website and materials look amazing but didn't cost the earth. Here, they tell us how they went about developing their logo and branding.

MM: How do you make sure you appeal to a wide customer base?

DB: Spinster's Emporium has a varied customer base due to the different products and services it offers. The customer statistics from the business show that the majority of clients are female, aged 25–34 and live in London. There is also a difference between the customers you attract and customers that interact via sales and social media.

The customer profile was originally based around me and my own needs and desires as a designer, I then used my other crafty/fashion friends as a focus group. But whenever Spinster's Emporium hosts events, I'm always really surprised by how diverse the customer base really is. The majority of customers at events and workshops have no creative background whatsoever and are people looking for creativity outside their daily lives. The business services them by supplying both materials and inspiration.

MM: Spinster's Emporium branding is very striking – how did this come about?

DB: Research, research, research. If you want to start your own business, then you need to research who your competitors are and why your potential new customers like them. Collect images of branding that you like such as photography, inspirational quotes, logos and packaging. Create mood boards to try and visualize everything together. The more information you can source, categorize and eliminate, the more money you will save by the time you have to call in the professionals.

If you are a creative person, then you are likely to have creative people around you – and if you don't, then network! The Spinster's Emporium website, brand concept, graphics and packaging were all created by friends or friends of friends in exchange for favours and/or discounts.

MM: Is it true that an illustrator created the Spinster's Emporium logo for you?
DB: Yes, but I had a very clear idea what I was looking for. Designers often have a difficult job trying to turn an imaginary idea into something that will be the identity of your baby. If you see some graphics you really like, then find out who the designer is and approach them for a quote.

The original graphics alone for the logo and website (not the build) cost around £600, but since then probably around another £1,000 has been spent. I also learned how to use Adobe Photoshop and Illustrator for myself and now do my own brand design development.

MM: You seem very clued up! Did you go on any courses?
DB: I went on a 12-week business course at The Hive, Nottingham Trent University's purpose-built Centre for Entrepreneurship and Enterprise. Anyone under 35 can apply; it is still free to everyone, not just local people or past graduates. At the end of the course I gave a presentation to a broad group of external business investors who absolutely loved my enthusiasm for what was then just a shop. One of them approached me after the presentation and said she was a branding expert and would like to mentor me. She taught me the important difference between developing a logo (short term) and building a brand (long term). I learned about the emotional relationship between the brand and the customer, and how establishing brand rules such as colour palette, tag lines and brand aims would become the backbone of the business's identity.

{ Top tips }

Donna Bramhall on branding

> If you are just starting out, organize your research, establish the brand identity, set goals and plan what you need to do to achieve them.

> Branding is not a logo: it is the experience you want your customers to feel inspired by when they interact with you.

> If you go to a networking event thinking how you can help someone else in a similar situation, it will come back to you.

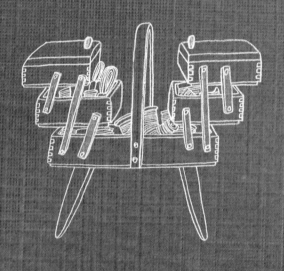

Chapter 2

Taking the plunge

Your company structure

Once you've made the decision to go full-time with your own craft business, you need to define its legal status. Sole trader, limited company or partnership: what do these terms mean and which is best for you?

In the UK, there are a number of options: you can set up as a sole trader, a partnership, or a limited company. This section gives a brief overview of the differences, but you should take proper legal and financial advice before making any decisions.

SOLE TRADER

Setting up as a sole trader (self-employed) is relatively straightforward, but you must register with HM Revenue and Customs (HMRC) within three months of starting your business. You do not need to register with Companies House. Being a sole trader means that you, as an individual, are responsible for the business; it does not mean that you have to work alone and cannot take on staff. You can use your own name or trade under a business name (see pages 16–17). Each year, you will need to fill out a self-assessment tax return (see page 140); failure to do this can result in penalties.

A sole trader is responsible for any losses that the business makes as well as keeping records of sales, purchases and spending. A sole trader will be required to send a self-assessment tax return; pay income tax on the profits the business makes; pay National Insurance (NI); and, if the business takings are to be more than £79,000 in a year, register for VAT.

Advantages

> The only paperwork you really have to do is your self-assessment tax return.
> You can manage your own affairs and may not need an accountant.
> The wage bill will be low, because there are few or no employees.

Disadvantages

> You have no one to share the responsibility of the business with.
> You will almost certainly find yourself working long hours and may find it difficult to take time off if you are ill or want to go on holiday.
> You will have to pay tax and national insurance on *everything* you earn. If you start doing really well, it may no longer be cost-effective to operate in this way.
> Your ability to borrow money is affected directly by your personal credit rating.
> You are personally liable for any debts that the business incurs and may have to pay them out of your own pocket.

LIMITED COMPANY

There are a number of different types of limited companies. The most common in the UK is a limited company that is limited by shares. There are three other types: limited by guarantee; unlimited; and public limited companies. A limited company has its own legal identity, independent of those who run it, and can sue or own assets in its own right. The ownership is divided into equal parts ('shares'). A limited company must be incorporated with Companies House and you must inform HMRC. There are a number of obligations that companies must adhere to each year, including: filing statutory accounts; completing an annual return; and sending HMRC a company tax return. As with a sole trader, if the business takings are to be more than £79,000 in a year then the company must register for VAT. Directors of limited companies are required to complete a self-assessment tax return and, if the company pays you a salary, pay tax and National Insurance contributions.

In a private limited company (ltd), shares do not trade on the stock exchange. Public limited companies (plc) are usually large, well-known businesses; they do trade on the stock exchange.

Advantages

> For a private company limited by shares, the shareholders' responsibilities for the company's financial liabilities are limited to the value of the shares that the shareholder holds.
> If you need to borrow money, the business will have its own credit rating.
> You will pay corporation tax, which, rather than being taxed on what you earn, is based on taxable profits.

Disadvantages

> There is more paperwork.
> You will need to employ an accountant and this could be costly.
> From a psychological point of view, many makers in the early stages of business feel this is a commitment they are not quite ready for.
> It is difficult and expensive to rearrange the ownership to change the profit sharing, introduce new owners or deal with resignations.

PARTNERSHIP

A partnership is a business owned by two or more people. It is similar to a sole trader business in that you do not have to register with Companies House and all partners have unlimited liability for the business's debts. If you go down this route, you will need to have a 'deed of partnership' drawn up stating how much capital each partner has invested and how the profits are to be shared.

One person must be a 'nominated partner' – the person responsible for keeping business records and managing the partnership's tax returns, which should show each partner's share of the profits/losses. The nominated partner must register the business for self-assessment with HMRC. All partners are responsible for their own tax returns and for paying their income tax and National Insurance contributions. Profits are not taxed before they are distributed to the partners.

There is also a form of partnership known as a limited liability partnership (LLP); in this, the LLP is liable for the full extent of its assets, while the individual partners' liability is limited. An LLP must be registered with Companies House.

Advantages

> All partners share the responsibility of running the business, so you can pool your skills.
> More people contribute capital to the business.
> You have someone who cares as much about the business as you do to consult about business decisions.

Disadvantages

> You may disagree about business decisions or argue about whether or not you are putting the same amount of effort into the business.
> Like a sole trader, all partners have unlimited liability (except in a limited liability partnership).

EUROPE

In mainland Europe, your local chamber of commerce will be able to answer many of your questions regarding setting up either as a sole trader or as a limited company. They will also be able to point you in the direction of organizations that can help you with registering your business. You will need to apply to join them before being accepted as a member but, in doing so, you will be able to take advantage of a wealth of opportunities, including networking.

UNITED STATES

Founded in 1953, the US Small Business Administration delivers loans, loan guarantees, contracts, counselling sessions and other forms of assistance to small businesses.

See also:
Restrictions on business names, page 17
Tax, pages 140–141
Public liability insurance, page 148
Employer liability insurance, page 149

FIND OUT MORE

> Gov.uk (www.gov.uk) is a good starting point if you want to set up your own business, whether as a sole trader, in partnership, or as a limited company.

> Companies House (www.companieshouse.gov.uk) is an essential site to bookmark if you're a limited company or thinking of becoming one. There is also a useful list of websites to register your company if you are based outside of the UK.

> Setting up in Europe? For the Netherlands register with KVK (www.kvk.nl); in Sweden register with Bolagsverket (bolagsverket.se); in Denmark register with the Chamber of Commerce, CVR (www.cvr.dk).

> In the USA go to www.sba.gov for information about setting up your business.

Home or away?

Now that you've taken the plunge and set up your business, where are you going to work from?

WORKING FROM HOME

To begin with, it's more than likely that you'll find yourself working from home – whether it be spread out on the kitchen table or, if you're lucky, from a summerhouse in the garden. However, there are some things you need to consider.

Mortgage and rental agreements

It is absolutely vital that you check you are able to work from home with your mortgage provider or your landlord before you do anything else. This is especially important if you have the sort of business that will require members of the public to come into your home or if you're working with equipment that could be seen as a fire risk.

Planning permission

This will not apply to most crafting businesses, especially in the very early days. However, if your home will no longer be used primarily as a private residence, or your business is likely to disturb the neighbours at unreasonable hours (for example, if you're going to be using noisy machinery), then you may need planning permission. If you're unsure, contact your local council. If you are planning to carry out building work to make substantial changes to your home, go to www.planningportal.gov.uk to find out if permission is required.

Insurance

When you're working from home it's easy to neglect insurance, but should there be a fire or burglary, you could find you're not protected.

First, call up your current contents insurance provider and tell them of your plans. It might be that if you're just using standard office equipment such as computers and printers, you already have a certain level of cover.

However, throw into the mix specialist machines and equipment and you may have to look at adding an additional policy to cover specific items. Most of the time you'll have the option to add this to your current monthly premium or indeed pay a one-off fee. Just make sure you know when it expires!

Health and safety

Although it's seen as decidedly unsexy, health and safety does not stop you having fun: it allows you to be creative but without the risks that could damage a fledgling business. If customers and suppliers are likely to visit you at home, carry out a comprehensive risk assessment of your premises and make any necessary improvements. The Health and Safety Executive (www.hse.gov.uk) will be able to help answer any questions you may have; for more information on health and safety requirements, see page 153. (In the USA visit www.osha.gov.)

CREATING A WORKSPACE

Once you've sorted out all your paperwork, it's time to start thinking about how you can create a space that's truly yours. If space is limited, choose a corner of a room that is bright and airy – better still, find a spot with an inspiring view. But unless you are in a studio apartment, stay clear of working in the bedroom you need to be able to relax there and this won't be helped if there's stuff all over the bed.

HOME IS WHERE THE MONEY IS...

A recent survey by the Crafts Council called *Craft in an Age of Change* (February 2012) reveals that some 65.9% of makers in the UK work from home, which, considering the economic climate around the world, is not at all surprising. It offers the convenience of being close to the kettle – and, should you wish to, you can work in your pyjamas! That's not to mention the financial aspects of having quite minimal start-up costs.

Whatever your business, a computer is essential, as is a printer; one that doubles up as a scanner and photocopier is particularly useful. Make sure you invest in a good-quality desk and office chair. Your own digital camera (see page 97) for photographing your creations is a definite asset. And a dedicated phone line and fast Broadband connection are must-haves.

TRY FOR YOURSELF

Different businesses have different requirements, so sit down and write a list of everything you think you might need – office equipment, any tools or machinery that you need to create your products, storage for all your bits and pieces and so on. Cost everything out and factor that in to your start-up costs (see Financing your business, page 46). Remember, you can always economize by buying secondhand equipment to start with.

STRIKING A BALANCE

It can sometimes be difficult to motivate yourself when you're working from home on your own – although knowing that you have to make enough money to pay the rent or mortgage every month is a pretty solid incentive! Although it might seem tempting to chill out in your pyjamas all day, getting properly dressed helps to get yourself in a workmanlike frame of mind. Starting work at the same time every day is also good discipline.

Instead of just 'commuting' upstairs to the spare bedroom every day as soon as you've finished breakfast, many people find it helpful to go for a short walk first: that way, not only do you get your daily exercise, but it also helps you to clear your head and get ready for what the day has in store.

In fact, getting the right balance between home and work is probably one of the biggest problems. When you're just starting a new business, you'll have to work long hours anyway, but try to make sure it doesn't completely take over your life. You need some time for yourself, too – not to mention your family and friends – so make a point of building that in. Put it in your diary, if you have to, in the same way that you would schedule a business appointment.

Still weighing up the options? Let us help you out with some pros and cons...

HOME WORKER

Advantages

> Relatively low start-up costs
> Most people have a corner they can designate as a workspace
> You can work around your home life
> You save money as there's no commute
> It's as quiet (or as noisy!) as you want it to be

Disadvantages

> It can be very lonely and hard to motivate yourself
> You could become distracted by housework and other tasks
> Separating home and work life can be tricky
> If you're making things, it can get very messy
> Expect to be disturbed by well-meaning friends who think 'working from home' means hanging around in your pyjamas

STUDIO DWELLER

Advantages

> You're likely to *feel* more professional, which increases productivity
> If your studio is within a creative hub, you will have other people to talk to and also support – like colleagues but you're not forced to sit next to them
> It's your own space and if you don't want to tidy up, you don't have to
> You'll be able to get much more organized, finding a place for everything
> If you want to invite people to do workshops, you can

Disadvantages

> It can be costly to rent a studio in addition to paying a mortgage or rent at home
> If it's some distance from your home you will need to commute, which can be costly in both time and money
> Committing to a contract can be difficult if you are yet to make a profit from your new venture
> Budget restraints can mean taking on a studio in a less-desirable location than you might like
> You have less control over security – for example, if you're in a studio with communal doors, you are relying on others to make sure they are locked

WORKING FROM A STUDIO OR RENTED OFFICE SPACE

Many makers are happy working from home for the whole of their careers, but if you feel you are outgrowing your home then, daunting though it may sound, it's time to look for a studio or office space to rent.

Approach renting a studio as you would a house viewing and draw up a wish list of your requirements. How much space do you actually need and can you fit all your equipment in there? Think about the facilities (phone line, Broadband, kitchen, toilet and so on) you're going to require. Are big windows and lots of natural light important to you? If you're thinking of doing lots of craft and trade fairs, is there a lift – or can you manage with just stairs? Struggling with boxes laden with goods could cause an accident and no one wants that! Can you park your car there or would you have to rely on public transport?

In addition to the actual studio space, you need to think about how working there might impact on you personally. How much time will you have to spend travelling every day? That's all time that will take you away from your creative work. And what about the general area – are there shops or cafés nearby that you can pop out to for a quick snack or would you have to bring everything in from home? Is it in a good location? If you're going to be working late some evenings, you need to be sure you would feel safe walking home or to the local train station.

If you're going to be having lots of bulky materials delivered there, you'll also need easy access for the delivery vans. If you're shipping finished products out, is there a post office nearby or will you be using a courier company who can collect from you?

Take a friend to see the place with you, as an objective opinion can be really helpful. If you get the chance to meet other occupants, have some questions ready to ask them as this will give you a real insight into what it is like to work there.

Last but definitely not least – can you really afford it? If you find your dream workspace, it's easy to get carried away in the heat of the moment – but renting a studio will mean a significant increase in your costs and all that extra money has to come from somewhere. Work out how much more you'll need to produce in order to cover those extra costs – or think about holding weekend workshops and tutorials there (perhaps inviting other makers as tutors) to help you recoup a sizeable chunk of your running costs (see page 128).

Once you're sure you've found the right place, make sure you fully understand the terms of the lease and what your obligations are as a tenant. Above all, take your time: this is a major turning point in your business and you mustn't let yourself be pressured into making a snap decision.

FIND OUT MORE

> The Crafts Council *Craft Directory* can be accessed online and provides comprehensive listings of organizations currently offering studio facilities. See: www.craftscouncil.org.uk/craft-directory/.

> Craft Central (www.craftcentral.org.uk) has a great reputation for springboarding the careers of successful makers. The 'in business' programme offers training and support to creative businesses at all stages of their careers.

> London makers may wish to visit Cockpit Arts. Makers here receive expert tuition and advice, in addition to studio spaces. Visit: www.cockpitarts.com.

> German artists may wish to visit www.bbk-kulturwerk.de/ for information about studios in Berlin.

> Another useful online resource is: www.transartists.org, which focuses on artist in residence opportunities in Europe.

> In the USA check local listings or online communities for information and advice about finding and renting studio space.

Mollie Makes talks to...
Louise Presley, artist and founder of Hope & Elvis

Louise Presley, artist and founder of Hope + Elvis (www.hopeandelvis.co.uk), works and organizes workshops run by established makers from her studio in Nottinghamshire. The place is full of items she wants to see repurposed and loved again. Louise talks to us about the benefits of having your own studio space.

MM: What's so great about having your own studio?
LP: There are lots of practical reasons why a studio is great: you don't have to tidy up at the end of the day and you have space for your creativity. For me, the main positive is having a dedicated space that I control. There is a sense of security in having all your work and accoutrements in one place, which also helps you to feel engaged and authentic. In my experience, doubt can feature in an artist's life and having a dedicated space makes you feel that you are indeed an artist and this is your place of work.

MM: So, it enables you to feel more professional?
LP: I guess what I am trying to say is that it validates your practice. It also helps to placate that gnawing doubt that you should really get a 'proper job'.

MM: Before having your studio, did you work from home?
LP: I had a space at home where I kept all my bits and pieces but in reality, it was just a place for me to store my collections.

MM: What is the best way to find a studio space in a particular area?
LP: I think you have to look at the traditional places first – arts organizations and the local councils – but tourist information centres, craft shops, galleries, shops and alternative education facilities all have good potential. I'm a firm believer in asking around, following your nose, rooting out possibilities and grasping opportunities! I have had three studios in

the last 10 years and all of these have been found by word of mouth, networking or recommendation. I didn't have a definite plan to have a studio but stumbled into one when I was encouraged by a buyer to approach a company with my work. They took all of my graduate fashion collection and offered me a space within their new country store in a Georgian farmhouse. I moved in within the week and set up an area to make bespoke clothing and a shop partitioned with a large 1930s sewing machine and it all snowballed from there! A change in personal circumstances meant I needed a space closer to home. Having joined an arts cooperative scheme launched by the county council, I heard of a free studio and then when I went to look at it, I heard of another one, and so forth.

MM: When viewing a potential studio space, what should a maker be looking for?
LP: There is a lot to consider when taking on a space; understanding your own needs is paramount. Work out what you need and look around as many places as possible. Consider the whole picture rather than the actual space. Is there a community or support network? Are there any restrictions, commitments or particular politics to consider? Do you need privacy and quiet to work or do you enjoy working in a shared environment? Is access important with opportunities to sell direct to the public? Does the location reflect your client base and aspirations? Don't jump until you are sure it fits with your needs.

MM: Why did you start inviting other makers to host workshops in your studio?
LP: As the business became established I could see there was potential to grow the audience and also keep a fresh offer for my regulars. Additionally, getting makers of repute helped raise the profile of the business generally. It took me years to pluck up the courage to write to Julie Arkell, but sometimes you just have to be brave. First and foremost, I only invite makers who I like, it's as simple as that. I believe it's not about what you make at a workshop, it's more about how you felt when you made it. I try to ensure that the day is a warm and positive experience for everyone and I have to be confident that my guest tutors will deliver this – but in return, I also try to make it a good experience for them and offer full support, always being on hand in the studio to help out.

{ Top tips }

Louise on successful studio working

> If you're thinking of inviting other makers to hold workshops in your studio, it's important you only invite people you admire.

> The pressure of rent can lead you to make decisions based on commercial gain, so be sure they are the right decisions and not just motivated by money.

> Working in a creative community such as a group of studios can stop you feeling so isolated.

Financing your business

You might be lucky and have the capital you need to fund your business or it might be that your start-up costs are low. If not, you might need to seek additional help – but before you do so, work out what your start-up costs would be.

The exact costs will obviously depend on the nature of the business. The items below are not a definitive list, but the general categories you should be looking at are:

> Raw materials and any specialist equipment you need to create your products
> Administrative costs (rent, utilities, phones, fixtures and fittings, insurance)
> IT and other technology costs (computers and software, printers, high-speed Broadband, website development and maintenance)
> Sales and marketing (marketing materials, estimated cost of advertising)
> Professional fees (legal and financial advice, membership fees for professional associations)
> Wages

Be as precise as you can about this; if you have to estimate, then it's better to overestimate. Take into account everything you will spend. If you're going to need three months from the time you sign a lease on your workshop to the day you can actually open for business, work out how much money you will need during those three months. Then add in your operating costs for at least 12 months ahead; it can take time for a new business to make regular sales, let alone a profit.

Still want to go ahead? There are a number of funding options and some will suit you better than others – a combination approach may work for you.

As well as working out your own start-up costs, draw up a personal budget – your rent or mortgage, food and general housekeeping expenses, household bills, car and running costs, clothing, entertainment, personal grooming, childcare, pension contributions, any other savings plans, any loan repayments and so on. This will let you see how much profit your business needs to make in order for you to survive reasonably comfortably.

PARTNER UP

Pairing up with someone can be a fantastic option for those who do not require total autonomy. Although mixing business with pleasure is not generally recommended, many makers have the financial backing of a spouse who is happy to help them get on their feet or even a friend who is good with numbers and looking for a return on their investment.

Partnerships work well when you've got a combination of skills – so if you lack expertise in a particular area, seek someone who has them. Don't limit your options to people you already know, however: joining a local networking group could widen your horizons. Your local chamber of commerce can be a great starting point for meeting someone outside your own circle, so get involved and sign up to as many networking events as you can to maximize your opportunities. For more on running a business as a partnership, see page 36.

SELLING SHARES

If you are setting up your business as a limited company (see page 35), you can sell shares to raise capital. There are different types of shares and they can have different sets of rights attached. Shareholders will acquire certain rights and will get a say in how a company is run, but this is likely to vary depending upon what rights are attached to the shares in question. Make sure you take proper legal advice.

THE BUSINESS OF BANKS

'I'm off to see the bank manager' is not an expression that fills most people with joy, but getting a bank loan to start your business can be a great option – providing you know exactly what is expected of you. And just because you've had an account with one bank for years, that doesn't mean you can't shop around and do business with another.

Borrowing money is a huge commitment and banks will need to see you are serious – draw up a comprehensive business plan (see page 50) before you even think about setting up a meeting. Make sure you know exactly how much money you need to raise, as you have to be able to justify every penny to a lender. Approaching a bank with vague questions like 'how much can you give me?' will not inspire confidence!

Be realistic about how much you need to borrow and the terms you think would work for you. Failing to meet the terms of your loan could not only damage your credit rating, but you could also lose any assets you have such as your business or even your home. On the plus side, most banks have small-business advisers that you can talk to if you have a business account or have taken out a loan with them.

GREAT GRANTS

Despite everything you read in the newspapers, there is still money out there. You just need to know where to look. The beauty of a grant is that you will not be required to pay this money back – but you will need to comply with certain criteria. It might be, for example, that all your marketing material will need to carry your funder's logo.

In the UK, the Arts Council (www.artscouncil.org.uk) is a good place to start to look for opportunities. Should your business be eligible for funding from them, it is straightforward to apply directly online. You should also look at www.gov.uk, where you can fill out a questionnaire and be directed to the most appropriate funders depending on the amount you need and the purpose.

You may also be eligible for a grant from the government, the European Union, and local councils and charities. However, there's always a lot of competition and grants are usually awarded for a specific purpose or project.

THE IN-CROWD

It might not be for everyone but 'crowdfunding' (or 'peer-to-peer funding', as it's also known) is becoming increasingly popular around the world with creative businesses. Crowdfunding is the practice of funding a project or venture by raising many small amounts of money from a large number of people, typically via the Internet. You come up with your business idea, which you promote via a platform website, and then people offer to help you fund it. The pitfall of this is that you may be required to offer some incentives, which could complicate things further. Used by both those looking for funding and those looking to fund projects, this approach might work for you.

Sweden's Funded by Me (www.fundedbyme.com) is a great example of crowdfunded initiatives and invites both entrepreneurs and investors to meet online and via social networking sites. The company's core belief is that it can be easier to have a handful of people commit a small amount of money than one person committing a large amount.

FIND OUT MORE

> Go to www.startupnation.com for a wealth of useful advice.
> Many banks' websites feature loan calculators to give you an idea of what is possible before you arrange an initial appointment. Check your credit score before you apply.
> Find business funding in your area using the British Bankers' Association's finance finder tool: www.businessfinanceforyou.co.uk/finance-finder.
> Go to www.smallbusiness.co.uk/financing-a-business/government-grants/ for information on government grants.
> If the idea of crowdfunding appeals, there's bound to be an initiative suitable for you. In addition to Funded by Me, there is also Funding Circle (www.fundingcircle.com) and Crowdcube (www.crowdcube.com).
> In the USA go to www.sba.gov for information about financing your business.

Writing a business plan

If you want to secure an investment or a loan, you will definitely need a business plan. And even if you're in the fortunate – and unusual! – position of not requiring additional finance for your business start-up, writing a business plan is still a good idea: it summarizes your business goals and how you plan to achieve them, so you can refer to it time and time again to make sure you're still on track.

You will already have thought about many of the topics in your business plan before you made the decision to go ahead with your business in the first place, but your business plan keeps everything together in one document. Writing it also helps you to focus on what's essential and may even throw up some considerations that you hadn't previously thought of.

If you're preparing a business plan for a bank or investor, aim for 20–40 pages of information. (If the plan is purely for your own use, you don't have to go into as much detail.) Your plan should be clear and concise, and backed up with all the research you've done. Use bullet points, clear headings, tables, graphs and pictures of products to get your points across, rather than expecting your readers to plough through reams of dense text. Above all, don't be overoptimistic in your forecasts; potential investors will expect you to be able to explain how you arrived at your financial projections and will quickly spot any flaws or weaknesses.

Each creative business is unique, so it's difficult to give a template here that will work for everyone. However, there are many free business plan templates available online and many of the organizations that support start-up businesses (see pages 48–49) can also give you invaluable advice on how to write a business plan.

WHAT SHOULD A BUSINESS PLAN INCLUDE?

> **Executive summary**: a synopsis of your entire business plan, highlighting the key points that you will cover in greater depth later in the plan.
> **Description of the business**: its legal structure, when you plan to start trading, your product or services and their USPs, how you plan to expand your range.
> **Market research and sales strategies**: your competitors and their market share, your target customers, the overall size of the market and the market share you aim to achieve.
> **Key personnel and their responsibilities**: include specialist advisers such as your accountant. This reassures potential investors that you have the right team of people around you.
> **Your operations**: your current or planned location and why you chose it, costs, IT systems and stock control.
> **Your finances**: forecasts of cash flow, sales, profit and loss for three to five years; how much capital you require; any other sources of revenue that you have; any securities that you have; any outstanding loans.

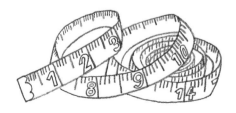

Emma Jones of Enterprise Nation

Emma Jones is the founder of small business network Enterprise Nation (www.enterprisenation.com) and the author of a number of books, including Spare Room StartUp, Working 5 to 9, Go Global and The StartUp Kit. We asked Emma about the challenges facing those who are thinking of starting up their own craft business.

MM: In the current economic climate, many people might feel wary of setting up their own business – even if they're sure they've got a really strong business idea. What would you say to them?

EJ: I'd say there's never been a better time to start a business! The costs of starting a business are at an all-time low and you don't even have to give up the day job, as you can do what I call 'Working 5 to 9', which involves building the business at nights and weekends and giving yourself time to build confidence and cash flow. There's also a lot of support available to start-ups and growing businesses, from crowdfunding to online forums, and lots and lots of practical workshops to help you on your way!

MM: In your experience, what are the main challenges facing new businesses?

EJ: The challenge of making sales! Many people attend my StartUp Saturday workshop and I can see they are brilliant at making their craft; what makes them nervous is getting the product to market. This has also become much easier with powerful platforms such as Etsy and Folksy and selling in person through craft markets and PopUp shops. See challenge as an opportunity and it will all fall into place.

MM: Getting funding for a new business is obviously critical. How would you advise people to go about doing this?

EJ: I'd say think carefully about whether you really need funding; most businesses I see start for less than a couple of hundred pounds and you can usually get that from friends and family. If you do need to access more, consider options such as StartUp Loans and crowdfunding on sites such as Kickstarter, Crowdfunder.co.uk and Seedrs.com. This is becoming incredibly popular as not only do you raise money, you also come to the attention of lots of customers. I've also written a free eBook on funding; go to www.enterprisenation.com/books/50-ways-to-find-funding-for-your-business.

MM: What do you look for when assessing someone's business plan?

EJ: The best businesses (and plans) are those that have a niche; by this, I mean they offer a particular product to a well-defined audience – so rather than offering all kinds of furniture, for example, a business focuses on making the best coffee tables for the small urban home. In doing this, you quickly become an expert in your field, you keep marketing costs low (as you know where your customers are, what they like, who are their influencers and so on) and you keep customer loyalty high, as customers can hopefully get what they're after from you.

MM: There's so much to think about when starting a new business. Where would you advise people to go for support and advice?

EJ: To Enterprise Nation! Seriously, we have lots of help from experts in the form of blog posts and eBooks and the community help each other at regular meet-ups. I also deliver StartUp Saturday, which offers all you need to know to start a business in the space of a day. I know I'm biased, but it's perfect for the craft business starting out!

{ *Top tips* }

Emma on business start-ups

> Come up with a niche idea.
> Find dedicated space in the house from which to work.
> Make a sale.
> Make some noise.
> Manage your money.
> Repeat!

Chapter 3

Creative
conundrums

Costs and pricing

When crafting is just a hobby, you probably don't worry too much about the cost of your materials. When it's a business, however, keeping control of your costs is paramount – and until you know exactly what your costs are, you can't work out how much to sell your products for.

WORKING OUT YOUR COST PRICE
Your cost price is how much it costs you to make one item in your range. There are a number of elements to consider.

Raw materials
List absolutely everything you use to make each item, from rolls of fabric right down to the tiniest snap fastener or scrap of ribbon.

Your time
This is the thing that makers seem to struggle with most. How long does it take you to make one item and how much are you going to charge for your time? Say, for example, you can make two necklaces in an hour and you want to pay yourself £15 an hour, then the labour cost for each necklace is £7.50.

Variable costs
In accounting jargon, both raw materials and the labour costs of making your goods are known as 'variable costs' – because the amount will go up or down depending on how many items you create. You may also see this figure referred to as COGS or 'cost of goods sold'.

Overheads
You also have to consider your overheads – things like rent on your workshop or studio, any equipment you need, phone and Broadband, the cost of electricity and other utilities, insurance, marketing materials, labelling and packaging and so on. You need to cover all these costs to

ensure that you are not operating at a loss. These are known as 'fixed costs' – they remain the same, no matter how many or how few items you sell.

Calculating your costs

Divide your fixed costs by the number of units you expect to create and sell over the same period of time. Add that figure to your variable costs, or COGS, and you know the true cost price for one item.

For example, say your raw materials and labour costs for one item come to £5.70 and you think you can make and sell 300 items in one month. Your fixed costs (overheads) come to £800 per month. Divide £800 by 300 and you get £2.66. Add £5.70 and £2.66 – this comes to £8.36.

This covers all your costs (assuming you sell all 300 items) – but all you've done is break even. To make a profit you have to add a mark-up to each item.

SETTING A PRICE

How much more should you charge over and above your cost price? You might come up with one price that works when you're selling for cash at a local craft fair. Sell the same item via an online portal such as Folksy or Etsy (see page 115) or from your website using PayPal, and you will also have to pay a small transaction fee on each item – so you make slightly less profit. Shops and galleries have to make their own profits, so they will buy from you at considerably less than the price you charge when you sell direct to customers.

Generally, you should aim for at least a 100% mark-up – that is, double the cost price. Ideally, multiply the cost price by 2.4 or 2.5. Shops vary, but most will work on the principle of a x 2.4 or x 2.5 times mark-up on what they pay you – so if you sell to them at £10, they will sell the item on at £24 or £25. (Bear in mind that the extra £14 or £15 is not pure profit for the shop: they have their own overheads – premises rental, staff costs etc. – to cover.)

Another approach is to work out what you think you can sell the product for and work backwards to see whether that gives you the profit margin you need – but you still need to know your costs in order to work out if you're making enough.

Allowing shops to order from you in bulk means you may sell more but at a slightly lower price per unit. Weigh up how much profit you're set to make and look at setting up a minimum order, whether it's for ten items or 100.

Make this work for you and don't be afraid to negotiate with the buyer – it's important to ask yourself if you feel it could be the start of an ongoing relationship or whether you foresee it as a one-off. Larger stores with a more established reputation may wish to place a small, introductory order to test the waters – if you're happy with this and feel it will benefit your business, don't be afraid to give it a go!

TRY FOR YOURSELF

Select one item from your range and work out the cost price. How much are you currently selling it for? Taking into consideration the time it takes you to make it, are you making a sensible profit? One of the most common mistakes people make – especially when they're just starting out and selling occasional pieces to fund their hobby – is to underprice their work. We're just so thrilled that someone – anyone! – actually likes our work enough to buy it. Do you need to adjust your own pricing structure?

OTHER FACTORS

In addition to your cost price, looking at what your competitors charge is essential and a useful exercise to see where your brand sits in the wider world. However, you don't want to pitch your price too high and price yourself out of the market; equally, there is no benefit in undercutting a competitor's price if you end up selling more but making less profit. Much of this comes back to your original market research and your product's USP (see page 13). Customers who buy handmade products expect quality and this should be reflected in your prices: a premium product will justify a premium price tag. Price something too low and your customers may feel that it is not of the finest quality or craftsmanship.

ONGOING PRICING CONSIDERATIONS

Once you've got your cost, retail and trade prices set, you'll have a much better idea of how to plan ahead and know exactly how much you need to sell to make your target profit. Monitor these regularly. In particular, keep your eye on the cost of your raw materials, as this is a key cost that must be accounted for if you are to grow your business year on year.

> Develop a pricing formula that works for you and stick to it.
> Be aware of price changes – both in the cost of your raw materials and in the wider economy. These will both have an impact on your profit and loss.
> Your pricing must always reflect your quality. If you make any products that are less than perfect, be sure to declare it. It is perfectly acceptable to sell these as 'seconds' at open studio events, for example.

SAMPLE PRICING FORMULA

Here is an example of a pricing formula used by crafters:

Supplies + Your time = Item cost

Item cost x 2.2 (up to 2.5, depending on how much you want to mark up) = Wholesale price

Wholesale price x 2.2 = Retail price

Sourcing raw materials

Finding and buying the raw materials you need is vital – but are you getting the best deal from your suppliers?

COST VS QUALITY

The chances are you already have a list of suppliers that you use regularly – but are you buying at the best price? Shop around, both in physical stores and online, and see if there's anywhere you could make savings.

Remember to compare quality, though. There's no point in sourcing cheap materials if the quality is inferior and a key component, such as the clasp on a necklace, breaks and you have to refund the customer their money. This not only eats into your profits, but can also lead to very unwelcome bad publicity for your business. A few negative comments on Facebook or Twitter (see page 82) can do a lot of damage to your reputation. In short, it's a balancing act between cost and quality.

BUYING IN BULK

A great way of saving money is to buy raw materials in bulk. Buying single items in your local craft store when you need them is fine when crafting is just a hobby – but if you can buy ten, or even 100, from a wholesale supplier, the unit price will come down considerably.

There is a caveat, here, however: although buying in bulk saves you money, it could tie up a lot of cash that you need for other things – particularly when your business is just starting out. Failing to anticipate and manage cash flow (see page 144) is one of the biggest problems for new businesses.

Base your buying on realistic forecasts of how many items you will sell over a given period of time. Keep a constant check on stock levels, and be ready to reorder at short notice if supplies are running low.

RELIABILITY OF SUPPLY

Make sure that your suppliers can fulfil your orders promptly and efficiently. Find out what their standard delivery times are – particularly if you're sourcing materials from overseas. If possible, try to have two or three suppliers of each component, so that you've always got someone to fall back on if your first choice lets you down.

VINTAGE SUPPLIES

There has been a huge resurgence of interest in vintage fabrics, jewellery and paper products and it is becoming increasingly difficult to find original pieces that you can repurpose in your own creations. Can you be sure you can source what you need to make the piece again?

If the material you're using really is a unique piece that you managed to track down on eBay or stumbled across at a vintage fair, make sure your customers know that it's a one-off piece that can't be repeated – and price it accordingly. Alternatively, see if you can make your vintage treasures stretch a bit further by combining them with reproduction 'vintage-style' components – without destroying your creative vision and what makes your products unique in the first place.

DEALING WITH SUPPLIERS

> With the Internet, new suppliers are just the click of a button away. One amazingly comprehensive source that allows you to find suppliers all over the world is Alibaba (www.alibaba.com). You can even restrict your search to specific regions of the world – so if you want to source everything in your home country, either to support your local economy or to avoid any potential problems with long shipping times, you can.

> Don't be afraid to negotiate and ask for a better price. Your suppliers will know exactly how much discount they can give while still maintaining a good profit margin – but if you don't ask, you probably won't get!

> If you're doing business with a supplier for the first time and placing a large order, don't be surprised if they want business credit references or insist on payment up front to begin with: they're in business, just as you are, and they can't afford to risk supplying someone who then doesn't pay up.

Mollie Makes talks to…
Sophie Simpson

Sophie Simpson is the designer, author and compulsive stitcher behind embroidery business What Delilah Did. From her little apartment in Norfolk, England, she runs a blog and online shop where she sells her distinctive cross stitch patterns and kits to customers all over the world, and to lifestyle shops and boutique haberdasheries in the United Kingdom.

MM: Deciding what to charge is something that a lot of craftspeople seem to have trouble with. How did you go about working out your prices?

SS: When I started out I just calculated my prices around the cost of materials because I wanted to be able to compete with mass-produced kits. That is fine if you are just selling a few things as a hobby, but impossible to sustain if you want to live off your craft business full time. I now have a two-part formula for my pricing where I work out the actual cost of selling the item (including raw materials, packaging, PayPal fees, etc.) plus the cost for my time in designing/producing it (as a percentage of my hourly rate), then round it up or down to the nearest whole number.

MM: When you first started selling to retail outlets, were you prepared for how much of a mark-up the shops would require? Did you have to adjust your own pricing structure as a result?

SS: I did a lot of reading before I started my business, but none of it prepared me for the mark-ups expected by retailers. Some of the largest stores sell your products for up to three times the price they pay you but still expect to keep their prices competitive, which makes it almost impossible for independent designers to get their foot in the door. In my experience the reality is that as a small designer/maker you are never going to make decent money from supplying large retailers, but they do offer the opportunity to get your brand seen by more customers than you could hope to reach on your own, so you really have to look at it as a marketing strategy more than anything else. You will often find that smaller independent shops have more reasonable mark-ups and are driven by more than just profit, so you can really build up a relationship with them as a supplier. In terms of pricing structure there is a limit to the amount of money a customer will pay for a craft kit, so I now produce a dedicated wholesale range that is quicker to put together and accommodates mark-ups, while leaving me free to make a wider range of individual kits for direct sale to customers in my own shop.

MM: Have you ever had problems with suppliers of your raw materials not delivering on time? How did you get around this?

SS: I may just be unlucky, but in my experience it is the exception rather than the rule for supplies to arrive on time/in the correct quantities. Because of this I always try to keep enough supplies on hand to cover me for a couple of months' worth of orders because I can't rely on them being available when I need

them otherwise. This is especially important if you are wholesaling your products to retailers because the chances are you will lose the contract if you can't fulfil an order on time.

MM: What are your top tips on pricing?

SS: As an independent designer/maker, time is your most precious commodity; do not undervalue it. I calculated an hourly rate for my time by working out how much money I need to live on per year, then adding to that all the general expenses of running my business over the same period (website fees, stationery costs, travel, premises costs, insurance, etc.) and dividing the total by the number of profitable working hours I have available in a year (keeping in mind that I spend at least half of my time on admin and other non-profit tasks). I use that hourly rate as a basis for all of my pricing. This may make your products a little more expensive than their mass-produced counterparts, but there will always be people willing to pay that bit extra for something truly unique, home-grown and beautifully made when it is marketed well, and if you don't account for your time you will just end up working around the clock with nothing to show for it.

Sophie's tips for pricing
> Don't undervalue your time – it is your most precious commodity.
> Calculate an hourly rate for your time and use this as a basis for pricing.
> Remember that you will only have a certain number of crafting hours available – your time will also be taken up by non-profit tasks, such as admin.
> People will always pay extra for something truly unique.

Staying inspired

Running your own business is all-consuming. There are so many things to think about – making the goods, stock control, invoicing, shipping, general admin. to name but a few – that it can be hard to find time for anything else. So how do you stop your creativity from going out of the window?

Be a magpie and collect snippets of anything that interests and inspires you! You never know what might spark off an idea for a new design – colour combinations that you just happen to stumble across while out shopping; textures that you see on your travels; flowers, pebbles, shells and other natural items; a photo of a far-flung location; a magazine feature about the latest fashions. Often, you may have no immediate idea of how you might incorporate it into your own work – but then weeks, or even months, later, something just gels in your mind and you're off and running.

Many makers and craftspeople keep notepads and sketchbooks permanently at hand, so they can make a note of things they find visually interesting. Rough sketches, photos, postcards, a few scribbled words as an aide-mémoire, even magazine cuttings: these are all useful reminders.

Other people find it useful to display items on a pinboard, where they're permanently in view; in addition to providing inspiration, it makes a great decorative display for your workroom.

The online equivalent is Pinterest (www.pinterest.com), which allows you to create a virtual pinboard where you and other people can view your favourite images. It's a great way of keeping all your sources of inspiration together, and you can organize your pinboards by theme. When you follow someone, their pins show up in your home feed – so if there's a designer whose work you particularly admire, or you simply want to see what a crafting colleague finds interesting, this is a great way to do it. Checking out other people's Twitter and Facebook accounts (see pages 82–83) is also a great source of inspiration – not to copy their design ideas, of course, but simply to keep yourself visually stimulated and up to date with current trends.

From a business point of view, you can also use these sites as a way of sharing your latest creations with your online followers (see Using social media, page 80): any pin on Pinterest, for example, can be 're-pinned' (added to another person's board), so your new creations can end up being viewed by countless other people who you may not actually know – a fantastic way of promoting your business.

KEEP UP TO DATE

Some craft businesses offer classic, timeless products – handmade, heirloom-style christening robes, for example. Others are more dependent on the vagaries of fashion: this year's cuffs and statement necklaces could well turn out to be next year's fluoro earrings!

If your business is based on current trends, make sure that you don't slip behind. As a creative person who has chosen to build their business in a particular area, you probably already have a good feel for what's on trend. But make a conscious effort to keep your eyes open and see what's going on in other fields.

For example, the fashions that originate on the catwalks of London, Paris and Milan generally filter down to the high-street clothing stores, but they may well go on to influence other areas, too. Metallic fabrics might be all the rage for eveningwear one season – and then you suddenly realize that metallic finishes are cropping up on home furnishings.

So keep an eye on what's happening on the high street. The stores have people who specialize in predicting trends – and this applies to homewares just as much as it does to clothing. If you see lots of a particular motif (animal prints, space monsters, roses in full bloom), or a certain craft seems to be coming back into vogue (remember how crochet underwent a massive revival after years of relative neglect), ask yourself if that's something you could tap into with your own products.

Making connections

Working on your own can be lonely at times, especially when you've got the stress of starting a new business to contend with as well. Fortunately, crafters tend to be a friendly bunch and you will find plenty of like-minded people willing to share their skills and expertise with you.

NETWORKING

Thanks to the Internet, you can connect with people all over the world at the click of a mouse. Many of the big online marketplaces such as Etsy and Folksy have forums that you can participate in. These cover both crafting and business-related topics, so you can share skills and ideas and get advice from fellow craftspeople on everything from craft techniques and sourcing materials to finding craft markets and pop-up shops, marketing ideas and getting paid. Even if you haven't got a specific question in mind, it's well worth browsing through them from time to time – they often contain invaluable information.

New social media websites seem to pop up every day and they're a fantastic way of making new contacts as well as keeping in touch with your old friends and colleagues. Many of you will already have your own personal Facebook and/or Twitter account, but you can also set up business accounts so you can keep your work and private lives separate.

And when it comes to networking, you really can't beat good, old-fashioned face-to-face contact! There are literally hundreds of craft groups out there, from informal 'Knit and Natter' groups to local branches of organizations like the Embroiderer's Guild, which host all kinds of interesting talks as well as giving you the opportunity to meet fellow enthusiasts, see what they're working on and swap ideas and techniques.

Finally, when you're out and about selling your work at craft markets, talk to other crafters and pick their brains – not just about what's selling well for them, but also about where and how they're selling. They may have come across a fabulous market or pop-up shop that you haven't heard of, or have some interesting marketing ideas that you could try out. Follow each other on Facebook and Twitter and, if their friends 'like' what they see of your work, you will soon begin to develop a much wider network of potential customers.

MENTORING

If you're looking for more formal support and advice, there are many ways of finding a professional who can mentor you and steer you through the sometimes tricky waters of running your own business. Mentors normally have extensive experience in a particular area, such as finance or marketing. They can be a great sounding board for your ideas and offer constructive and impartial feedback based on their own business experiences.

See also:
Selling online, page 114
Craft fairs, page 106

FIND OUT MORE

> Overwhelmed and not sure where to turn? You can access business advisers through your local chamber of commerce, your bank or even your former university.

> If you're looking for a business mentor (or would like to become a mentor yourself), go to www.mentorsme.co.uk. You can specify what stage your business is at (start-up, growing or established) and your region and find listings of business mentors in your area.

> Another useful contact is the National Enterprise Network (www.nationalenterprisenetwork.org).

> The Enterprise Programme of the Prince's Trust (www.princes-trust.org.uk) offers mentoring support to unemployed 18 to 30-year-olds if their business ideas are viable.

> In the USA go to www.sba.gov for information about finding a business mentor.

Mollie Makes talks to...

Cat Morley, founder of Cut Out + Keep

Cut Out + Keep (www.cutoutandkeep.net) was founded by Cat Morley in 2003 while she was still at university. Begun as a blog, it is now an online community that allows its users to create and share crafty projects that include knitting, crochet, baking, papercraft, and even wirework. We talked to her about her business and the importance of online networking.

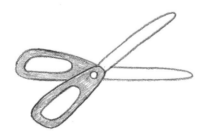

MM: How did Cut Out + Keep come about?
CM: After adding over two hundred of my own projects, my partner Tom decided to make a system so I could easily add step-by-step instructions. We soon realized this could be a great resource for other crafters, so we opened up the site so that anyone could share projects. Neither of us imagined it could grow so big and become a resource for so many people.

MM: Who are the main users of the site?
CM: We have members all over the world, but the majority are in the USA (85%), Canada, Australia and the UK. North America is definitely our biggest demographic. Readers are almost 100% female.

MM: Is there a need for creative people to share things online?
CM: I think that creative people have always felt a need to share their work and get feedback, but now the Internet provides an easy way to get feedback from friends and like-minded crafters around the world instantly. More importantly, it's also a great way to find inspiration to encourage you to start a new project and source help and tips along the way.

MM: Do you think the Internet offers more possibilities for crafters than ever before?
CM: Yes! The Internet is changing so many different industries and ways of life. For makers, it provides more information to learn new skills, a way to make creative friends and be inspired. It also provides a platform to share your work with a global audience without limitation. For some people, the idea of selling to a worldwide audience is a motivator to craft more.

MM: Your site includes many inspirational projects. How do you create a really good step-by-step tutorial?
CM: Take lots of photos and try to be as detailed as possible when explaining difficult steps.

MM: What advice would you give someone who was setting up a website?
CM: Keep the design simple and clean, so it's easy to navigate and fill it with really great content, so that readers want to come back time and time again.

Cat on creative networking

> You don't need a friend or relative to teach you skills any more. If you want to find out how to make something, get online.

> When you look up instructions for a particular craft online, allow yourself to become part of a virtual community.

> If you've made something and are looking for instant feedback, you will find it online and you'll be able to connect with people who live thousands of miles away.

Expert advice from…

Hayley Banks of Design Factory

Hayley is membership manager of creative development organization Design Factory (www.designfactory.org. uk). Originally established to support makers in the East Midlands, it now offers programmes called Fresh and Fusion for those outside the area, and a global audience of 8,000 makers receives their newsletter. We asked Hayley what benefits they can offer.

MM: How does a maker qualify for your support?

HB: Membership is independently selected by a panel of industry specialists and offers six levels of subscription tailored to develop the creative practice of emerging, new, mid-career and established designer/makers. In 2012, we introduced a formal mentoring scheme and in its first year this has provided mentoring support for eight emerging designer/makers and valuable mentoring experience for eight of Design Factory's Fellows (established designer/makers).

MM: What opportunities are open to your members?

HB: Members can showcase their work at prestigious regional galleries and through group stands at national trade fairs such as 100% Design, Top Drawer and Pulse. A growing international programme also provides designer/makers with valuable research and development, trade, export, cultural exchange and commercial exhibition opportunities in Japan, Denmark, France, Germany and New York. Depending on the level of membership, makers will have an initial one-to-one meeting or telephone call to discuss their business and creative practice and this will result in the development of an 'action plan'. We also provide training events to address particular issues such as pricing, marketing and business planning, using experienced facilitators and subject experts.

MM: What are your success stories?

HB: Since 2009 we have supported an exhibitor group at the Maison & Objet trade fair in Paris. As a result our members have made sales and received orders from all over the globe, including large corporate orders from Japan, Australia, India, Saudi Arabia and the USA, as well as from across Europe. Design Factory was invited to showcase members' work in an exclusive exhibition at a central Paris gallery in 2011 and members now list prestigious outlets such as the Christian Dior design boutique among their stockists.

Hayley's tips for running your business

> Immerse yourself in the craft and design world by visiting galleries, exhibitions and trade fairs.

> Talk to other makers and ask for their advice.

> Use social media to research other makers and find out about opportunities.

> Subscribe to specialist publications such as *Crafts* and *craft&design* magazine.

> Be ambitious and don't be afraid to take risks.

> Apply for as many opportunities as possible and aim high in terms of seeking outlets and exhibition opportunities for your work. If you have the confidence and commitment to grow your creative practice and make a name for yourself, then you will succeed!

Protecting your intellectual property

They say that imitation is the sincerest form of flattery – but if someone directly copies and sells your designs or uses your trademark, it can have a serious impact on your business. So what can you do to stop this from happening?

Copyright, trademarks, design rights and patents all come under the heading intellectual property (IP). If you protect your intellectual property, no one else has the right to use it without your permission – and if you give your permission, you have the right to charge them to use it. The UK Intellectual Property Office (IPO) has lots of information on its website that explains the differences and provides sample agreements and other documentation (www.ipo.gov.uk).

Copyright

Copyright protects written works, illustrations, photographs, computer software, film and sound recordings and work that appears on the Internet. Knitting and sewing patterns, for example, would be protected by copyright, as would your blog. You do not need to register copyright: copyright protection is automatic as soon as the work physically exists. Mark your work with the copyright symbol (©), your name and the year in which the work was created. In the UK, copyright lasts for 70 years after the death of the copyright holder; the figure varies in other countries, but is usually at least 50 years (25 for photographs).

As there is no official register of copyright, you need to be able to prove that you're the owner. One option is to put a copy of the work in an envelope and mail it back to yourself by special delivery (so that there's a clear date stamp on the envelope). Leave the envelope unopened in a safe place; if a dispute over copyright arises, you then have the proof that the work existed on a particular date. Alternatively, lodge a copy of the work with your solicitor.

Trademarks

A trademark is the means by which a business makes itself visible in the marketplace. A trademark cannot be used to stop competitors from making the same goods or from selling the same goods or services under a clearly different mark, but it does provide a means of addressing the use by other people of your trademark or a confusingly similar mark.

Trademark registration in the United Kingdom grants the owner a statutory right to prevent others from using the trademark without the registered owner's permission. When you apply to register a trademark you must specify the goods or services in relation to which the mark is to be used by reference to the registry's listed 'classes'. There are currently 45 established classes of goods and services. These are listed on the IPO website.

Unregistered trademarks are protected through the tort of 'passing off'. It is generally more difficult to successfully win a claim for passing off than a claim for infringement of a registered trademark.

INTELLECTUAL PROPERTY INSURANCE

You can take out insurance on your intellectual property to help cover your legal costs in the event of you taking someone to court. If you go down this route, make sure that the insurance company specializes in IP – it is a complicated area and outside the scope of most general insurance companies.

Design rights

Design rights protect the three-dimensional shape of something original that you design – a piece of jewellery or a sculpture, for example. There are two types of design rights – registered and unregistered. Registered designs can last for a maximum of 25 years. The duration of protection is five years initially, but it can be extended every five years for a further five years. For more information, contact the IPO or Anti Copying in Design (ACID).

There is also a stronger form of design right protection in the UK, which does require registration through the IPO. Registered designs do include two-dimensional patterns. To register in the EU, apply to the Office for Harmonization of the Internal Market (www.oami.europa. eu). Outside the EU, for countries that are members of the Hague Agreement, apply through the World Intellectual Property Organization (www.wipo.int/hague); for countries that are not signatories to the Hague Agreement, apply to the relevant government department in that country.

Log on to the IPO website for information on how to show that your intellectual property is protected.

Patents

Patents are to protect inventions. If you come up with a completely new gizmo for automatically sorting piles of beads into different sizes or a totally revolutionary design for a kiln, for example, you can apply to register a patent. The process can be a lengthy and costly one, so it is best suited to ideas that have really huge market potential.

UNITED STATES

The United States Patent and Trademark Office (USPTO) and the United States Copyright Office lead the protection of intellectual property in the USA. As in the UK and Europe, different types of intellectual property are protected by different means:

1. Patent protection, which applies to inventions, designs or plants, must be sought by application to the USPTO.

2. Trademarks protect words, names, symbols, sounds or colours that distinguish goods and services from those manufactured or sold by others and to indicate the source of the goods. Registration with the USPTO is not required, but does provide certain advantages.

3. Copyrights protect original works of authorship, including literary, dramatic, musical, artistic and certain other works, both published and unpublished. In the United States, the United States Copyright Office handles copyright registration that, although not required for protection, does confer advantages.

RESOLVING IP DISPUTES

If you think that your intellectual property rights have been infringed, you should get in touch with the person concerned and either get them to stop or draw up a commercial agreement whereby you grant them permission to use or sell your design in return for payment of a licensing fee.

Make sure you put everything in writing. You can either write to them yourself or get a solicitor or intellectual property lawyer to contact them, although you really should seek legal advice before you take any action. If a strongly worded letter fails to bring any results, the IPO offers a mediation service. As a last resort, you may have to pursue your claim through the courts – a costly and stressful experience for everyone. If this happens, be sure to use a specialist legal adviser who understands the ins and outs of IP law.

FIND OUT MORE

> Visit www.gov.uk/browse/business/ intellectual-property or www.ipo. gov.uk.

> You can download free guides to IP from the World Intellectual Property Organization (www.wipo.int).

> The British Library Business and IP Centre in London (www.bl.uk/bipc) offers information and workshops on the best form of intellectual property for your business.

> ACID (Anti Copying in Design), provides legal advice, mediation in disputes, workshops and a wealth of useful information.

> For sample copyright infringement letters, go to www.nssea.org/ resources/copyright_infringement_ letter.cfm.

> In the USA visit www.uspto.gov and www.copyright.gov for information.

Mollie Makes talks to...
Gillian Harris

Gillian Harris is the author of Complete Feltmaking and Carnival of Felting and has been felting for over 15 years. She used to be a graphic designer, but her crafting business grew organically from 2001 into Gilliangladrag Ltd. She now runs a full-time business that includes a shop, a studio for teaching and a busy website, www.gilliangladrag.co.uk.

MM: Your business has grown dramatically over the years. Tell us about it.

GH: I established my business not long after the birth of my second daughter. With my family's roots in tailoring and the rag trade I was very pleased to pursue my love of textiles and then fell into feltmaking. In 2010 I moved our flourishing feltmaking business from my home into its new headquarters, 'The Fluff-a-torium'. We sell a wide range of products; there is a studio above for teaching felting, knitting, crochet, sewing and embroidery, and we also sell kits and craft items to businesses around the world wholesale too. We have a busy website too, which obviously allows us to sell to customers all over the world.

MM: Have you taken any steps to protect your designs from being copied?

GH: I have always tried to protect my designs with ACID (Anti Copying in Design).

MM: How did you first find out your designs had been copied?

GH: I saw one of my bag kit designs in a trade magazine but in a different colour. Other than the colour everything else was the same – and the maker had been one of my students, so I knew it wasn't just a coincidence!

MM: What was your reaction?

GH: I was shocked and totally devastated. I felt foolish for imparting so much information to this student – but then at the same time I enjoy teaching and sharing my knowledge – so that will always be a dilemma. Ultimately however, I decided that if people feel the need to copy your designs publicly and for monetary gain, then they clearly have a shortage of their own ideas. Sometimes it's best to try to ignore 'mild' copying and concentrate on your own ideas and focus on your own business. 'Getting justice' can be a negative and exhausting process, and I soon realized that because the person copying me had made a few colour changes with the design, she would get away with calling it her own. Sometimes it feels like there is no justice in such matters!

MM: What advice would you give to anyone who finds themselves in a similar situation?

GH: I would definitely recommend protecting your designs as best you can. ACID were helpful as they have their own team of lawyers who will help and guide you through the process without incurring huge legal fees. The person in question was warned to make her designs sufficiently different so as not to cause confusion in such a small niche market. Also be aware of intellectual property rights and what you are and aren't covered for. Some people (including large companies) can be very underhanded, and it only takes a few minor changes on a design for them to legitimately call it their own.

MM: What additional precautions should you take when selling your designs in different territories?

GH: Obviously be aware that different countries are bound by different legal processes, so your designs and products may be protected in one area of the world, but not another. It might be a lot more difficult to bring about legal proceedings for intellectual property rights in countries you are not familiar with. If you are unsure, it is important to get legal advice about the particular area you will be selling in – or take a view not to worry about it too much!

{ *Top tips* }

Gillian's tips for protecting your intellectual property

> Register your designs and the date you designed them.
> Join an official copyright 'body' such as ACID – it's worth the money.
> Keep your eye out for people who are mimicking what you are doing, and also for clear carbon copies.
> Take action if necessary.

Chapter 4

Spreading the word

Using social media

One of the greatest things about the Internet and social media is that they allow you to promote your brand and products all over the globe – and at very little cost other than the amount of time and effort you choose to put into doing so.

Blogging, Pinterest, Facebook and Twitter are all really easy ways of advertising and telling regular customers what you're up to. You can use them to let people know about a new product line, or give them snippets of background information that help to make you stand out as a really inventive and original craftsperson, or promote the fact that you're going to have a stall at a local craft market the following weekend, for example.

BLOGGING

A quick Internet search will reveal lots of companies offering build-your-own-blog templates; some are free, some are not. If you've never blogged before, talk to other crafters and see which ones they've used and whether or not they would recommend them. It really is incredibly easy to set up a blog: just go to the website of the blog-template company you've chosen and enter your details under 'create account'. You'll then be able to enter your data, and upload your pictures and/or videos. You can also choose whether or not you want your visitors to be able to add comments – a fantastic way of getting feedback and being part of a bigger crafting community. All that's left for you to do is write your entry and hit 'publish' – and your blog is there for all to see.

POPULAR SITES THAT OFFER FREE BLOGGING
www.blogger.com
www.livejournal.com
www.wordpress.com

Writing a blog

Some people use their blogs as an online diary, packed with details that have no bearing on their business – who they've just had lunch with, what cute antics their pet kitten has got up to, even (heaven forbid!) that they had a bit too much to drink the night before. If you owned a shop on your local high street, you wouldn't dream of sharing that kind of information with everyone who walks in – but that is effectively what you're doing when you put it in a blog.

Of course, the whole point of blogs is that they're personal, friendly and unique – but if the intention is to promote your business, your blog must put across the right image of you and your brand (see page 16).

(see page 16)

TRY FOR YOURSELF

Do a Google search and log on to five crafters' blogs that you haven't looked at before. What impression do you get when reading them? Are they the work of a lively, dynamic designer who's constantly trying out new ideas and is passionate about what they do? Does the look of the blog complement the company image? Now ask yourself what impression you want to convey in your own blog and think about how you can achieve that.

So what should you write about? First, make sure it's relevant to your business in some way. For example, your five-year-old's school nativity play probably won't interest most casual browsers – but if your business is customizing clothes and you designed all the costumes, then it would be appropriate to mention it in your blog. Equally, include anything that shows that your business is going places – if you've just landed a big order from a prestigious retailer, shout it from the rooftops. And people love getting insights into your creative world – what you're working on at the moment, those gorgeous fabrics that you bought on holiday in the Far East, those charity-shop finds that you're planning to transform into funky, one-off pieces and so on.

In short, put yourself in your readers' shoes: what do they find interesting and what will keep them coming back to read (and hopefully buy) more from you? Reading visitors' comments will help you with this.

Once you've set up your blog, make sure you update it regularly; it's a good idea to set aside a regular time every week, or every fortnight.

If you're not a natural wordsmith and feel daunted by the whole idea, try to forget that you're writing something for other people to read. Sometimes, people try too hard to write 'proper' English and it can all end up sounding a bit forced and stilted. Instead, imagine you're talking to someone who has just stopped by your stall at a craft market. Keep things chatty and friendly, think about the kind of questions they might ask you – and don't get bogged down in too much detail.

FACEBOOK, TWITTER AND PINTEREST

All these are free to join and use – although, if you are planning to use them from your mobile phone, you should check the cost of any Internet usage or text messaging with your network provider. You'll find more information about Pinterest on page 64. The chances are that you already have a personal Facebook and/or Twitter account, but if the whole thing is new to you, here's how to get started.

To sign up for Twitter, go to www.twitter.com, key in your name, username (which must not have any spaces in it), password and email address, and click on the 'create my account' button. The next page that you see will be your home Twitter page; type your message (which must be no more than 140 characters) into the text box, click 'update' – and lo and behold, you've sent your first 'tweet'.

To sign up for Facebook, go to www.facebook.com and enter your name, birthday, gender and email address into the form, then pick a password. You'll receive an email from Facebook; click on the link to confirm that you own the email address in question. You'll then be asked to verify your account, which will allow you to take advantage of more of Facebook's features.

To sign up for Pinterest, go to www.pinterest.com and click 'Join Pinterest'. Choose whether you'll sign up using Facebook, Twitter or your email address (although you can only link to a personal Facebook page, not a business one). Enter the username, email address and password you want to use for Pinterest, then click 'Create Account'.

There isn't space here to go into issues such as privacy settings, how to post content on your Facebook page, and so on, but there is a wealth of information available online, on both Facebook and Twitter's own websites and elsewhere.

Getting people to follow you

Once you've joined, you can 'follow' (on Twitter and Pinterest) or 'like' (on Facebook) other people, which means that their updates will appear on your home page. But from a business point of view, the main aim is to get people to follow you. Here, quality is better than quantity any day of the week. Focus on getting followers who are genuinely interested in your products or skills, and are therefore more likely to become customers.

Start by following people in the same field as you – other crafters, designers whose work you admire, craft show organizers and so on. The chances are that at least some of them will start to follow you in return.

Mention your Pinterest, Facebook and Twitter accounts in all your printed sales and marketing material. For instance, you could say something like, 'Follow us on Facebook for our latest special offers'. Finally, make sure you have links to all your social media accounts on your website and blog.

SOCIAL MEDIA TIPS

> Make sure your Twitter and Facebook names are the same as your business name, so that people make the connection.
> Don't make your Twitter username too long, as it counts as part of the maximum of 140 characters that is allowed when someone is tweeting you.
> Can't fit what you want to say into 140 characters? Then put the information on your website or blog and link back to it on Twitter.
> Be sure to include your social media account details on your website, blog, business cards and any other marketing material you create.

Although we've concentrated on marketing here, you'll soon find that you can use your blog and social media to benefit your business in all kinds of ways. Canvassing opinion on new products, building up customer profiles, finding out about new suppliers or techniques, discovering new sales outlets, sharing advice on creative and business matters... the possibilities really are endless.

Mollie Makes talks to...
Jane Foster

Jane Foster runs the eponymous Jane Foster Designs in Totnes, Devon, selling Scandinavian-inspired quirky toys, cushions and bags that she screen prints herself. She is the author of Fun with Fabric and has had several of her screen prints and designs published as posters and cards. We talked to her about how she uses social media in her business.

MM: Your website looks really fresh and lively – just like your creations! How did you go about designing it?

JF: Thank you! I discovered a really cool local website company in Totnes called VU. I clicked with the team immediately and felt they understood me and my work. We worked together to produce a fun, easy-to-use site. They were brilliant at converting some of my designs into my own brand with a cool logo and moving eyes, cat, and so on for the home page. I wanted to be able to get behind the scenes to add my own product photos while they do the more technical side of things such as the moving photo headers on the main page.

MM: Your blog is always up to date and interesting! How much time do you spend on it – and how do you decide what to write about?

JF: I try to add new entries three or four times a week, spending around 10–15 minutes on it. I don't like writing too much, so I keep it mainly to photos of what I've been doing or what has inspired me. I also like to add photos of the processes I use – for example, photos of my drawings and screen printing. And I like adding photos of fabric I collect and photos of around our home and my studio, as people always like to peek behind the scenes! I don't tend to write about other people's work in my blog, as it would take up too much of my time.

MM: Do you think your Etsy shop drives traffic to your own website?

JF: Yes, definitely – especially from shops that want to contact me to sell my products wholesale. This is mainly where I'm spotted by people in other countries.

MM: How important are social media sites like Facebook and Pinterest to your business?

JF: I think they're very important. I wish I'd started both of them years ago, but I wasn't very clued up. I also think that I felt they would be too time-consuming (which is partly true!) and at the time, I was also juggling a toddler!

Starting Facebook and Pinterest has helped my business a lot – I'm able to show photos of my latest designs and people can be directed straight to my website or blog. It's also a great way of doing research on who is following me, what country they live in and what age group I'm mostly reaching. I also get to see what kind of posts create the most comments and feedback – this will help me to see which products that I'm designing are more popular than others. I love the fact that Facebook is a real community and you start to get a sense that you're not the only one passionate about fabric, Scandinavian design, etc. You can almost feel you're making new creative friends, even if you're never likely to meet them in person! However, social media is very addictive so you have to be disciplined and only spend a short amount of allocated time on it, even though it's tempting to browse other people's blogs and Facebook for hours. Having real deadlines usually helps me to be motivated to get back to work!

MM: Some crafters can be a bit technophobic when it comes to social media. What's your advice to anyone struggling to get to grips with it all and make it work for their business?

JF: As a starting point, pay an expert for half an hour so they can check your settings are safe and give you some guidelines. They'll also help you to upload photos, have a link to your website and remind you of good social-media etiquette.

{ Top tips }

Jane on using social media

> Keep posts brief and positive: never moan in them!

> Use good, eye-catching photos.

> I think it's very important to reply and thank people for any comments they leave, especially if they've added lovely long ones! This can be very time-consuming, but I think it's good netiquette!

> If you've got a new product you want to show and you'd like it to reach lots more people, you can pay a small fee to boost your post so more people will see it.

> Add some humour into some of your photos so that people know you're not just completely work-mad!

> Include the odd photo of behind the scenes, perhaps of your home or workspace, as people love to see your environment.

PR material

Away from the wonderful world of the web, there are more traditional ways of promoting your business, from simple business cards and brochures through to press releases that you can send out to magazines and retailers.

It goes without saying that all your PR material should have a unified look, so that people can easily identify it as being yours (see Building your brand, page 16). Although you will have to invest a certain amount of money, it may not be as expensive as you might think.

BUSINESS CARDS

Good-quality business cards are essential. If you don't want to go to the expense of having them specially designed and printed, there are lots of companies that allow you to drop your own imagery into a ready-made template. Be sure to include your email and website/blog addresses, your online shop if you have one, and your Facebook name or Twitter handle.

Always, always take a few business cards with you wherever you go, even if you're just popping out to the shops or the gym: they take up next to no space and you never know when you may find yourself chatting to someone who wants to find out about your products or services. You can't expect them to memorize your name or website address – and jotting the information down on the back of an old supermarket receipt isn't going to give a very business-like impression.

When you make a sale, why not slip a business card in with it? Yes, it may get thrown away when the customer gets home; alternatively, they may like your work so much that they hold onto it for future reference or pass it on to a friend.

LABELS AND STICKERS

PR is all about keeping your business name at the forefront of your customers' minds. Look inside any item of clothing from your wardrobe and what do you see? A label with the name of the shop or company that made it! Is this a ploy that you could use on your own products?

And have you thought about branding your packaging? Why not invest in some custom-made rubber stamps or stickers with your business name and contact details?

PROMOTIONAL POSTCARDS AND FLYERS
These give you space for far more information or imagery than you can fit onto a business card. Obviously they're more expensive to produce, so you won't necessarily want to give them out to all and sundry, but if you've got a special promotion coming up or are bringing out a new line, they're well worth considering.

If the cost seems prohibitive, why not share it with someone whose work complements your own? Print your details on one side of the card and your friend's on the other – and you'll both have access to a wider network of contacts than you would as individuals.

BROCHURES AND CATALOGUES
As your business grows and you start looking for magazine coverage and exhibiting at trade fairs, you'll need a more detailed brochure or catalogue to show to potential buyers. In addition to your contact details and information on how to order, for each product you'll need a great photo, a brief description, different size and colour options (if applicable) and a product code or item number.

Your catalogue will be going out to people, retailers and journalists and their response to it can have a huge influence on the success of your business, so (unless you have great graphic design skills), you'll probably need some professional help. To be sure that you brief your designer properly, take time to think about the look that you want.

If you're likely to be selling the same range of goods for some time, you might like to consider having a separate price list that can be slipped inside, so that you can change your prices if you need to.

Writing a press release

You don't have to be a Pulitzer prize winner to write an effective press release, but something that's carefully targeted, well written and to the point will have much more chance of being followed up.

The golden rule is to keep it short – preferably just one A4 page (300 words or so). If you find that you're having to write far more than that, you've got an article on your hands, not a press release!

As far as your writing style goes, that too should be punchy, so aim for sentences that are no longer than about 25 words. Remember that the purpose of a press release is to give news, so keep it factual and not too flowery. Don't make exaggerated claims or hype things up too much – journalists can spot that kind of thing and they won't be impressed.

Don't use lots of exclamation marks or put words (or even whole sentences) in capital letters in an attempt to draw attention to them. In printing and publishing jargon, exclamation marks are sometimes called 'screamers' – and for good reason. Overusing them is the literary equivalent of standing in front of someone and shouting in their face.

Above all, make sure that your product or event is relevant to the publication in question: there's absolutely no point in sending a press release about customized bead necklaces to a magazine that concentrates exclusively on knitting!

Although the publication will edit the press release and even rewrite it in their own style, take the time to check the facts and proofread it before you send it out. Spelling mistakes and bad grammar look sloppy and unprofessional.

STANDARD PRESS RELEASE FORMAT

Use letter-headed paper or put your company logo at the top of the page and write 'Press Release' underneath; you might think it's obvious, but journalists and editors receive all kinds of material – press releases, internal memos, sales figures, and much, much more – so they need to be able to tell at a glance what they're dealing with. Then follow the format below:

Timing – for immediate release or under embargo?

If you're happy for the information in your press release to be used straightaway, write 'For immediate release' followed by the date you sent the press release; most press releases fall into this category. If you want to keep things under wraps for a while (so that your competitors can't steal a march on you, for example), write 'Embargoed until…', followed by the relevant date.

Headline

Don't fall into the trap of starting your headline by saying 'Joe Bloggs announces…'. This not only makes the headline impersonal and overly long, but it's superfluous: the reader already knows who you are from the logo or letterhead. Instead, write a snappy headline that will grab the editor's attention and make your press release stand out from all the others he or she receives on a daily basis.

First paragraph

Keep it short – ideally no more than 60–70 words. The test of success is whether the story can be understood in its entirety from just this first paragraph. The advice generally given is that this paragraph should try to answer the following questions (although some are perhaps more relevant to events or campaigns than to new products):

> Who? (Who are the key figures involved? Who does your news benefit?)
> What? (What are you telling people about that's new?)
> Why? (Why is this important news? What does the product or event provide that is different?)
> Where? (If your press release is about an event, where is it taking place? Is the location of your business relevant?)
> When? (When is the event taking place or the product becoming available?)

Subsequent text

The rest of the release should consist of just two or three more paragraphs, giving further details. Including a quote here can be a good way of making your press release more colourful, but make sure it's relevant and has authority. For example, a generic 'customers say...' won't necessarily carry much weight – but if an industry specialist is willing to endorse the product, or a respected source backs up your claim that the market for this type of product has increased dramatically, then the quote would have some validity. After the last paragraph write 'Ends' in bold type.

Contact information

Give the name, address (physical and email) and phone number of the person the journalist should contact for any further information.

PHOTOS

Good photos always help; in fact, many stories appear as just a photograph and caption.

If you do include them with your press release, don't send too many – and make sure the files are small enough not to clog up the editor's email inbox, as that's a surefire way NOT to win friends. You can always add a note at the bottom of your press release saying that high-res versions of the photos are available on request.

As with the text of your press release, study the publication to find out about the style of photos they use. If you're aiming to get something featured in a round-up of interesting products or gadgets, then cut-out white-background shots (see page 103) are probably what's required. If the magazine is more of an aspirational, lifestyle publication, then a beautifully styled shot might be appropriate. If in doubt, contact the editor and ask what they're looking for.

MAKING IT!

Press Release for Immediate Release – October 2014

Exclusive new products for knitaholics launch at Making It! for Autumn 2014

A new collection of Making It! knitting needles are now available. The covetable collection has been designed to help beginners and master crafters to produce beautiful fashion items to knit, stitch and wear with pride. These exclusive items complement the brand's impressive range of luxury yarns and knitting patterns. The full product range is available from the Making It! online store at www.makingit.com and London-based boutique, Making It! Emporium.

Knit into fashion

The Making It! collection of deluxe wooden knitting needles offers crafters the chance to make the latest knitwear patterns in style. Each pair of needles is embellished with a hand-painted design featuring a delicate blossom motif. The range is available in 16 different sizes (from 2.25mm to 10mm) and a variety of colours. Each pair is sold in a matching cotton case, so you will always have a safe place to stash this season"s must-have knitting accessories. Prices start from £5.99.

About Making It!

The design-led knitting brand, Making It!, was founded in 2014 by Mollie Maker. From luxury yarn to knitting accessories, the brand sells everything crafters needs to create beautiful handmade knitwear. – 'Making It! products will be adored by everyone living and loving handmade'. (Mollie Makes).

ENDS

For product samples, high-resolution images, interviews with Mollie Maker, or any other general press enquiries please contact Mollie Maker, email: molliemaker@makingit.com, tel: 12345-678-910.

Feature articles

Getting a magazine or newspaper to do a feature on you or your work is priceless in terms of the amount of interest it can generate. You may be lucky enough to have a journalist approach you directly, as a result of having seen your blog or website, but don't be afraid to make the first move.

The key is to go to them with a ready-formed idea – a 'hook' on which a writer can build a story. Obviously, it has to be something that the magazine's readership will find interesting, so look at previous issues to see what kind of topics are covered.

Try not to focus exclusively on your product range: you need to come up with a story that people will want to read, not an advertorial. If you make handmade bags from recycled clothing, for example, then (rather than concentrating on the bags themselves) a good angle might be how you're doing your bit for the environment. If you use silk paper made by a cooperative in the Far East in your designs, the story might be how you discovered the cooperative, or your account of a recent trip there, or how the operation has given the women of the village some degree of financial independence.

Another option is to offer to create a project specifically for one of the many craft magazines on the market. As with any kind of feature, do your research and pitch the project at a technical level that the readership can relate to.

Find out who is the best person to send your idea to. You can generally do this by looking at the masthead – a list of the key staff, which is usually placed at the front of the magazine. If you draw a blank with that, phone up the switchboard and ask who to send feature ideas to. In your covering letter or email, make a point of addressing the person by name rather than just typing 'Dear Editor'.

Be organized. Keep a list of all the people you've contacted, the feature idea, and their response. It may take a while for them to get back to you, but if you haven't heard anything after six weeks or so, drop them a line asking if they've had a chance to look at your idea – but don't be too pushy. If they haven't replied after a couple of emails from you, the chances are that they're not interested – although that doesn't mean to say that other ideas of yours would not work for them in the future.

TRY FOR YOURSELF

Draw up a 'hit list' of four or five publications that you think your work might be suitable for – either for a step-by-step tutorial or a feature article. Include at least one that isn't specifically aimed at crafters – a general women's interest magazine, perhaps, or a local newspaper. Analyze the kind of topics they cover and think about what kind of 'story' you could pitch to the editor.

LEAD TIMES

Magazines work a long time in advance, so you need to bear this in mind when sending out press releases or pitching an idea for a feature. It's no use sending them something that relates to Christmas at the beginning of December, for example: the Christmas issue of a monthly magazine will be on sale from early November and the contents will have been planned quite some time before that – so for Christmas features, you should ideally approach the magazine no later than the start of the school summer holidays! In publishing jargon, this is known as the 'lead time'.

Expert advice from...

Ruth Bonser of British PR company, Rumour

Rumour (www.rumourpr.com), which concentrates on the design and craft industry, was set up by friends Ruth Bonser and Mel Lee, who met while working in PR and marketing at British brand Cath Kidston. Here, Ruth explains why good PR is vital.

MM: Why should makers spend money on PR?

RB: If you have created a great product and brand, you need to tell people about it. The world is full of fantastic craft companies; to set yourself apart from the others you need to shout about yourself a bit. PR, to put it simply, is placing your products and story under the nose of your potential customers. It is important, as you can't just rely on people stumbling across it by accident.

MM: What exciting brands have you worked with and what's been achieved?

RB: We were so excited to work with the lovely Kay Mawer, owner of the iconic craft company Clothkits. We managed to get the Clothkits story told in the Saturday Telegraph magazine, which prompted a huge response in readers who remembered the brand from the 1970s.

We also worked with the modern knitting and yarn company Millamia on their launch, which was a bit of a dream for me as I am a huge fan of anything knitted!

Another hugely successful craft company that we work with at the moment is Buttonbag, who create knitting, sewing and other kits for children. It's so important to pass the love of craft and the skills down through the generations and Buttonbag kits are perfect for this.

And last but not least, we have Catherine Tough, who has grown her love of knitting into a very strong brand, creating beautiful, modern knitted goods that are sold throughout the world and online.

MM: What do you offer that individuals cannot do themselves?

RB: We are constantly talking to the right magazines and have a huge network of contacts in the industry. There are five of us in the office, working on both PR and marketing for around ten companies. If you have a craft company, it is likely that your time is filled with product development, wholesale, logistics, finances, and all the different elements that make a company work. Using a PR agency is often cheaper and more effective than employing someone in-house to do it, especially if you are a growing company.

MM: What is the best way to create a 'buzz' around a product?

RB: The best way, in my experience, is getting the timing right, which is using all your promotional tools to talk about the product at the same time. First, make sure you have sent the information to the press early enough so they can consider it for a feature at the time you want to launch it. Then when the press starts coming out, email your database with news on the product launch. This would be the right time to start your social media campaign around the product too – so Twitter/FB/Pinterest/blogs, etc. – any press coverage, photo shoots you have done, customer feedback and photos, etc. By bolstering the press coverage with your own marketing to your customers, you are getting your product seen in as many different places as possible.

{ Top tips }

Ruth on PR on a budget

> Good photography is the most important aspect – it's rare to get into any publication without a picture of your product. Decent cut-out photography (on a white background) and ideally a nice styled shot is preferable – and always high resolution, otherwise it will be too small for print.

> Do your research – thoroughly read and get to know all the magazines and newspapers you think your customers would read, and work out which section you would fit into. Find out who writes those sections (it's not hard with a bit of investigation), and send them a friendly email introducing yourself, keeping it visual and brief. Most craft/homeware writers are a friendly bunch and if they think your product is interesting enough for their readers, they will put it in.

> Don't be disheartened if you don't hear back – just try a different tack with a new product another time.

> Blogs, online magazines and social media are becoming just as important as printed media for PR coverage – and often generate more sales. Get yourself into the craft blogosphere by reading and commenting on like-minded blogs, and you'll gradually create interest in yours.

> Twitter is excellent for making PR contacts: we find it essential to keep up with what magazines and journalists are working on.

Getting professional PR help

When you're first starting out and every penny counts, hiring a professional PR person might seem like a luxury that you can ill afford – but is it?

Whether you've just started your own business or have been running it for several years, there are always many demands on your time and skills, particularly if you're working on your own. Designing and making your products, sourcing materials, keeping your website up to date, managing cash flow, dealing with customers and retailers – not to mention keeping a balance between your work and home life: it's no wonder that PR sometimes takes a bit of a back seat. The hours that you spend honing a press release or emailing magazine editors might just feel like the straw that's going to break the camel's back. And let's face it – sometimes you may simply be too close to things to be objective.

Few new businesses can justify the cost of hiring a PR person as a full-time member of staff, but there are lots of agencies and freelance PR specialists out there who you can pay on a job-by-job basis.

The benefit of hiring a professional is that they're used to writing snappy, eye-catching copy. They have a bulging address book full of useful contacts and know exactly who to go to, what each magazine's lead time is, and what kind of features they're likely to be interested in. Conversely, magazines will be dealing with someone they already know and trust, rather than a novice who may not fully understand their deadlines or requirements. All this helps to build the image of your company as a professional, go-getting enterprise. Good PR will help raise your profile with consumers and with professionals (such as the all-important buyers); it also breeds confidence in your brand.

A professional can put together a coherent marketing and PR campaign and may well come up with ideas that you'd never have thought of, leaving you free to work on other areas of your business.

As with everything, you need to weigh up the pros and cons. It's a good idea to at least try doing your own PR, so that you understand the processes and start to build up your own network of contacts – but don't assume that professional PR is going to be too expensive.

Photographing your products

Good product shots are essential – and you don't have to be a professional photographer or own a top-of-the-range camera to take them.

EQUIPMENT

These days, technology is so good that you can take great shots on a fairly simple compact camera or even a smartphone. For more creative control, however, go for a compact that has several modes to allow you to shoot in different lighting situations (indoors, outdoors in bright sunlight, outdoors in overcast conditions) or, better still, a digital SLR. It is possible to hire cameras, lenses and other equipment by the day (go to www.calumetrental.co.uk or www.hireacamera.com), but the costs can rack up quite quickly, so you're probably better off investing in your own. If your budget is really tight, consider borrowing a friend's camera or buying one secondhand.

You don't necessarily need lots of expensive lenses; a short zoom (say, 28–135 mm) should cover most eventualities. Most modern zoom lenses also have a macro (close-up) facility, which is useful if you're likely to be shooting very small items such as jewellery.

Two other really useful pieces of kit are a tripod to hold the camera steady and a shutter release to fire the shutter remotely, so that you don't risk jolting the camera and ruining your shot.

Add in a few pieces of white card to use as reflectors to bounce light into shaded areas of your shot, and a piece of white gauze or linen fabric to diffuse the light on a really bright sunny day, and you're good to go!

GETTING THINGS SHARP

With most compacts, there really isn't all that much you can do to change the depth of field (the area of the image that is sharp). Here, we'll assume that you've got a digital SLR.

The area of the image that is in sharp focus is controlled by the size of the aperture – the hole in the lens that allows light through to the sensor. The smaller the aperture, the more will be in focus. (Confusingly, the smaller apertures are the ones with the bigger numbers: f/22 is small while f/2.8 is big.)

If you want more of the image to be really sharp, use a small aperture; if you want a creative out-of-focus effect in part of the image, use a large one.

However, if you adjust the aperture, you will also need to adjust the shutter speed in order for the same amount of light to reach the sensor – otherwise your image will be under- or overexposed. If you make the aperture smaller (by changing it from f/8 to f/16, for example), less light will reach the sensor so you will need to leave the shutter open for longer. If you make it bigger (by changing it from f/11 to, say, f/5.6), more light will reach the sensor so you will need to reduce the amount of time the shutter is open.

If you use your camera in aperture priority mode, you set the aperture you want and the camera will adjust the shutter speed accordingly, so you don't have to worry about it. The main reason for choosing manual mode over aperture priority would be if you need to use a particular shutter speed – for example, a slow shutter speed to blur moving water or a really fast shutter speed to freeze the action. With product shots, this isn't likely to be an issue – so go for aperture priority.

TRY FOR YOURSELF

Find something like a long-stemmed flower or a twisted length of ribbon and place it on a table angled away from you, so that it will run diagonally across your image from bottom left to top right. Place your camera on a tripod and take a series of shots from exactly the same position at different apertures and shutter speeds – for example, 1/500th of a second at f/2.8, 1/60th of a second at f/11, and 1/15th of a second at f/22. How much does the area in focus change?

GETTING THE EXPOSURE RIGHT

Modern camera metering systems are pretty good, but there are some situations where they can be fooled and give an exposure that is either too dark or too light. Once you understand why this happens, it's fairly easy to put it right.

Basically, cameras are programmed to assume that there's a full range of tones, from white through grey to black, in everything they 'see'. If you're photographing something very light in tone – a white christening robe, for example – the camera will assume that a large part of the white area should actually be grey; it will make the white darker to achieve this and the image will be underexposed. If you're shooting something on a background of black velvet or slate, it will again assume that a large part of the black should be grey – so it will make the black lighter and the image will be overexposed.

To get round this, you can either leave the shutter open for longer or use a bigger aperture – both of which will allow more light to reach the sensor. However, changing the aperture may well have an effect on the depth of field (see Getting things sharp, page 97). Some cameras have a feature called 'exposure compensation', which allows you to increase or decrease the exposure in smaller increments than you can achieve by making changes to the shutter speed or aperture; this can be useful if very fine adjustments are needed.

Another way of getting whites to look really white is to use the camera's built-in white balance control; consult your camera manual to find out how to do this.

CHECKING AS YOU GO

If your camera has one, you can use the depth-of-field preview button to check your images during the shoot; then, if you don't like what you see, you can reframe or adjust the shutter speed or aperture to get the effect you want. However, it's sometimes hard to tell exactly what you've got until you put the image onto your computer screen. Another option is to link your camera to a laptop so that you can review images at a larger size; you have to take the memory card out of the camera to transfer the images onto the computer, so it does slow things down a bit.

With digital SLRs, you can also check the histogram on the back of the screen to make sure you've got the exposure right.

NATURAL OR ARTIFICIAL LIGHT?

Shooting in natural daylight reduces the likelihood of colour casts from artificial lights – and you don't need a really bright, sunny day. If possible, don't use flash as, unless you really know what you're doing, this can cause really harsh shadows or overexpose part of the image, and can look very unnatural.

PROPS AND BACKGROUNDS

The type of props you choose obviously depends on the kind of product you are selling and the look you are after – shabby chic, shiny and hi-tech, grand and elegant, young at heart, vintage, contemporary... the possibilities are endless.

If you think you're going to be doing product photography on a regular basis, it's worth building up a props store; you probably already have lots of things in your home that you could use, such as nice china and tablecloths, but car boot sales, junk shops and charity shops are all good sources of inexpensive props – not to mention being great fun to rummage around!

You could also incorporate some of the tools that you use – particularly if they're beautiful objects in their own right, like vintage scissors or chisels that have a well-worn, craftsman-like feel to them. They can really help to convey that you're an artisan with a specialist skill.

Similarly, you could include some of the materials you use in your products. Things like ribbons and lengths of lace trim are great: not only do they look fabulous, but they can be made to twist and turn through the shot, adding a sense of movement to what might otherwise be a fairly static image. Piles of buttons, reels of cotton or skeins of embroidery thread, strings of pearls or semi-precious stones are other options.

TRY FOR YOURSELF

Look through magazines, catalogues and at online suppliers and pick out shots that you really like. Ask yourself *why* they work: how do the props relate to the products that are being sold? What camera angle has the photographer used? How much space does the product take up, compared to the props and background? If you can train yourself to analyze photographs in this way, you'll be well on the road to taking successful shots of your own.

Whatever you choose, think about the scale of your props in relation to the item you want to showcase. The props add mood and atmosphere, but they are incidental to the shot: the product itself is what you want people to focus on. When it comes to props, less is more!

Like props, the background should complement, not distract from, the products. Contrasts in texture often work well – metal jewellery on soft velvet, pretty silk scarves draped over the edge of a gilt mirror. Does the background relate directly to the product? For example, you could give a hint of a rustic bathroom setting when photographing sweet-scented soaps and bath products, or place 1920s-style glassware on a period chrome tray, or arrange folk art-style hand-painted boats on pieces of driftwood.

The key to good product photography is to take your time. Don't snap away frantically taking hundreds of almost identical shots in the hope that one will be a winner. Professional photographers spend ages making tiny adjustments to their still-life set-ups before they ever press the shutter – and even then, they'll review the image carefully to make sure they've got exactly what they want.

COMPOSITION

Instead of just plonking your product down in the centre of the image, try to direct the viewer's eye to it in some way. Our eye will naturally follow lines that lead in towards the focal point, whether they're actual objects (paintbrushes pointing in towards a piece of hand-painted china, for example) or implied lines. It often works well to place your main subject 'on the third' – but make sure it's large enough in the frame.

FILE FORMAT AND RESOLUTION

Digital SLRs give you the option of shooting in different file formats. The very largest ones (RAW files) take up a lot of memory and take up space on your computer. To be honest, unless you're planning to shoot a photo to use on an advertising hoarding you generally don't really need to shoot files this big: large JPEGs are more than enough for most purposes.

More important is the question of resolution. It's advisable to shoot high-resolution files and reduce (or compress) later, depending on how you're going to use the image. If the images are for a website, you'll only need 72 dpi (dots per inch); for print, you'll need around 300 dpi, which is still a long way below the highest-resolution files that you can shoot. Bear this in mind if you're emailing photos of your products to magazines; the editor really won't be very impressed if you completely clog up his or her inbox! You can always email a low-res file and tell them that a higher-res image is available should they need it.

Incidentally, if you're going to do any work on your images in Photoshop or another program, make a copy of the original and work on the copy; every time you open and resave a JPEG file, you lose a certain amount of data.

FLARE

This is when you get a small but distracting patch of light on an object. It often happens with glazed ceramics. Try placing a piece of white gauze between the subject and your light source. The light is then diffused through the fabric, eliminating the flare. Alternatively, you can use a light tent. Placing an object inside a light tent allows direct or hard light to be diffused as it passes through the fabric of the tent and then to be further softened as it is reflected around inside the tent.

UNWANTED REFLECTIONS IN SHINY METAL OR GLASS OBJECTS

Changing your camera angle can help, but it's almost impossible to eliminate such reflections completely. If you're shooting something very small from close up, you could also try cutting a hole in a piece of black card for your lens. Stick the lens through and take your photos – the reflection will then be of a black surface with a small, dark round hole, which may not show up as much. For larger subjects, another way of minimizing the problem is to make sure that there's nothing brightly coloured or highly patterned in front of the object; go for neutral, paler colours instead. (It's worth thinking about this in relation to your clothing, too: all too often, you take a shot only to find you've got your own reflection in it!)

BLURRED IMAGES

Even the steadiest hand can still produce blurred images. Using a tripod is especially important for product photography since product shots often use slow shutter speeds. An inexpensive tripod will produce clearer product shots than a shot taken with a hand-held camera. To completely eliminate motion blur from your images, one solution is to use your camera's self timer or remote control. Even when a camera is mounted on a tripod there is some movement at the time the shutter button is pushed. Using a self timer or remote control will eliminate that motion.

WHITE-BACKGROUND SHOTS

Often, magazines want shots on a plain white background to use in new-product review pages, so it's well worth having these on file as well as more highly styled images. The easiest way to set these up is to pin a large sheet of white paper to the wall, allowing the bottom half of the paper to rest on your table top; place your product on this and you'll have a seamless, non-textured, crease-free background. Watch out for distracting shadows, though!

Think really carefully about your camera angle. It's often best to shoot straight on, with the camera level with the subject. If you photograph something like a tall, thin bottle from a higher vantage point, you may well find that the bottle appears slightly distorted and seems to narrow towards the base. Look at other product shots to see what viewpoint the photographer has chosen – and review your shots really carefully to make sure no distortion has occurred.

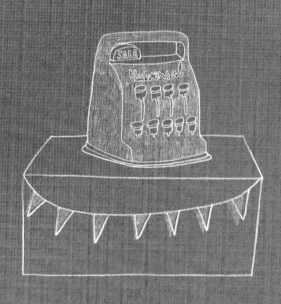

Chapter 5

Sell, sell, sell

Craft fairs

The chances are that your first foray into selling your creations will be at a local craft fair. It's a great way to test the waters: you can get feedback on your products, iron out any glitches in your presentation and packaging, and network with like-minded people, all without risking too much financially – and it's a fun day out, too!

FINDING FAIRS

Your first challenge, of course, is to find a fair to sell at. With the massive upsurge of interest in all things handmade in the last few years, this is now easier than ever before. It seems as though the world and his wife are jumping on the crafting bandwagon: as well as groups of crafters setting up their own fairs, the organizers of schools and church fêtes and even cafés and pubs are recognizing that well-made crafts can draw in members of the public who might not otherwise have paid them a visit.

PROMOTING YOUR BUSINESS

Advertising and promoting a craft fair is not solely the organizer's responsibility: make sure you play your part in promoting it as extensively as you can. Be sure to mention it on Facebook and Twitter and in your blog (see pages 80–83), both before and after the event. Offer to hand out leaflets. Ask if you can put up posters at your place of work, library, gym, hairdresser's, local shops – in short, anywhere you think there are people who might be interested in attending. You could even put a small flyer in the back window of your car.

Aim to visit fairs that happen on a regular basis as a customer first, so that you can see the set-up for yourself. That's by far the best way to get a feel for how busy they're likely to be and what kind of things sell.

By the time you see an advert for a one-off craft fair in your local paper, it's likely that all the stalls will have been taken – so how do you track down those elusive money-spinning opportunities?

Networking is key. If you're involved with your local church or have kids at school, you will find out about any fêtes well in advance; ask friends and family members to let you know about events at their school or church, too. Talk to fellow crafters, both face to face and in online forums, read their blogs, and follow them on Facebook and Twitter to find out where they're selling. Keep an eye out for regular events in your area – many towns have craft fairs once a month, often tying in with the local farmers' market. Peruse the noticeboards in your local arts and crafts shops, and even the supermarket – anywhere you think people might advertise such an event. Google 'craft fairs in [name of your area]' and see if anything comes up.

TRY FOR YOURSELF

If you're new to craft fairs and still holding down a full-time job while you dip your toes into the crafting waters, research what's on in your area. Once you've established the ones that will suit you best, set yourself a target of one craft fair a month. This will give you time to make new stock to replace what you've (hopefully!) sold, assimilate the results of your market research, and adjust your pricing and product range if necessary.

IS THIS THE RIGHT FAIR FOR YOU?

There are good craft fairs and bad craft fairs, and ones that work for some crafts but not others – so how do you sort out the wheat from the chaff?

First, ask yourself if your particular craft is suitable for the fair in question. If you're producing high-end ceramics or designer textiles, for example, then you're probably not going to sell much at an event that's geared more towards being a family fun day, with fairground rides and a bouncy castle for the kids. Similarly, if it's being promoted as a fine-art show, then knitted and crocheted toys won't be what most visitors are looking for.

How much is the stall going to cost you and how much will you have to sell to recoup that money? If it's expensive and you're selling mostly small items such as greetings cards, then you're going to have to sell a lot just to break even. But if you're selling one-off pieces of designer jewellery, then a single sale can be more than enough to justify the financial outlay.

Think about the location, too. Is it near a busy town centre, where passers-by will come across it even if they haven't seen any prior advertising, or is it tucked away down a back street, with little or no chance of attracting passing trade?

Here's a quick checklist of things to ask the fair organizer:

> How long has the fair been running and how experienced are the organizers? (You might want to phrase this a little more diplomatically!)

> How much is the stall and is a table and chairs included in the price?

> If it's outdoors, is there cover in the event of bad weather or do you have to bring your own?

> If you need extra lighting such as spotlights, can they provide it? And if you can bring your own, is there access to power points?

> Do you need to take out public liability insurance or have any other licences or permits? (See pages 148–149.)

> How many people are they expecting to attend?

> Where and how are they advertising the event?

> Is anyone else selling products similar to yours? Experienced craft show organizers will make a real effort to get a good range of crafts – both to give the customers variety and also to ensure that stallholders aren't competing directly with each other – but it's always worth asking the question.

> Can you park nearby?

> Can you buy food and drinks at the venue or do you need to bring your own?

> What are the trading hours and do you have to stay until the very end? If things are quiet, it's sometimes tempting to pack up early – but some shows don't allow you to do that as it's not only disruptive for other vendors but it also gives a really bad impression to any late customers if half the tables are empty.

There may be things you need to add to this list, but these are the basics for any craft fair.

> Stock to sell (obviously!) – make sure everything is clearly labelled with the price.
> Table and chairs, if not provided.
> Tablecloth; for outdoor fairs, it's also worth taking clips to hold the cloth down if it's windy.
> Gazebo for outdoor fairs (if the organizers aren't providing cover).
> Display stands, bowls, baskets, 'props' to make your display more appealing.
> Paper/plastic bags for you to wrap customers' purchases in; for delicate items, you may also need tissue paper.
> A plentiful supply of business cards.
> Notebook and pen to jot down customer feedback or commissions.
> Food and drink for the day.

SETTING UP YOUR STALL

Your stall is like your shop window, so make sure you display your goods attractively. Have a trial run at home, so that you're not still agonizing over your display when the first customers arrive.

It's tempting to set out as many items as you can, but a cluttered table makes it more difficult for people to home in on the key products and you can end up with something that looks more like a jumble sale. Be selective: if you have the same item in several different sizes or colourways, for example, only put a few out to begin with, then replenish your display when you need to. You can always tell customers that you have other sizes and colours available if they seem interested.

Make sure your tablecloth is big enough to cover the table completely and hang right down to the ground at the front; this hides any unsightly boxes and packaging that you might have behind the stall. And choose a neutral colour, without any pattern, so that it doesn't distract from what you're selling. Velvet is a good choice: it has a lovely, soft texture that catches the light well and it doesn't crease.

If possible, try to arrange items at different heights rather than having everything lying flat on the table. Depending on your craft, there are lots of purpose-made display stands that you can use – but if you can't find anything suitable or don't want to invest too much to begin with, improvize by placing sturdy boxes on the table and draping fabric over them to create shelves at different heights.

Other display options include wicker baskets and trays (great for giving a country-style feel to your display), slate or even small pieces of sun-bleached driftwood (jewellery looks fantastic on either of these), and big shallow bowls for small items like hair bands and fabric brooches. A collapsible rail is virtually essential for clothing, as is a print rack for photos, prints or unframed paintings – but check with the organizer that there's going to be enough space for it alongside your stall.

In the early days, you probably won't want to splash your cash on expensive signage – and at small, low-key fairs this really isn't necessary. As you move on to bigger and better things, however, it might be worth investing in a banner with your business name and logo, so that you immediately stand out from the crowd. Another thing to consider is having T-shirts or aprons printed with your logo – again, this reinforces your brand and identity.

You will also need to think about the forms of payment you are prepared to accept on your stall, such as card payments or Internet-based systems like PayPal or Sage Pay. For more information on these options see pages 142–143.

ORGANIZING A CRAFT FAIR

If there are no regular fairs near you, why not organize one yourself – either on your own or with a group of fellow crafters?

Obviously, your first task is to find a venue. Church halls and community centres often hire out rooms and, as they're always well used by the local community, you've got a ready-made customer base there. Moreover, they have kitchen and toilet facilities, so you might be able to operate a small café there on the day – an added incentive for people to come along and browse.

Other options include cafés and pubs – perhaps not an obvious choice, but a craft fair could be a good way of attracting customers in at a time when they'd normally be quiet. You could get your stall holders to pay their pitch fee direct to the venue, so they're making money and you're taking no financial risk.

Make sure that the stallholders pay you well in advance. You could offer them a discount for prompt payment or for booking several fairs at the same time; this will encourage people to book early, so you'll know a long time ahead how many tables you still have left to fill.

It's up to you whether you want to vet applicants to make sure their work is of a high enough standard, but be wary of having too many stalls that are just selling on goods they've bought in. Keep a note of what each stallholder is planning to sell and make sure you don't end up with too many similar products. Tell the stallholders exactly what they're getting for their money, where the venue is and where they can park, what the set-up time and procedure is, and when the fair ends.

The venue will almost certainly have its own public liability insurance, but you should check whether you (as the organizer) and the stallholders need to take out any additional insurance. Make sure, too, that any stallholders who are selling food-related items provide you with copies of the necessary food hygiene certificates.

Advertise the fair in any way you can – Twitter, Facebook, flyers in local shops and so on – and get your stallholders to do the same. If the fair is going to be a regular occurrence, contact your local newspaper and see if they'll run a feature on it (see page 92). If you're getting a banner made to hang at the entrance to the venue, time-proof it! Instead of putting the date, say 'Craft fair this Saturday', for example. Posters and banners can be an effective way of advertising, but if you want to put up banners on a public road you may need to get permission; check with your local council.

Finally, follow up by asking your stallholders for constructive feedback after the event; they'll be happy to give it, as it's in everyone's interests to make any future events a success.

Mollie Makes talks to…
Sinead Koehler, Crafty Fox Market

Sinead Koehler runs Crafty Fox Market along with her husband, Stephan. The ethos of Crafty Fox is to support and promote designer/makers. Sinead and Stephan also run Crafty Fox Talks – a series of speaker-led evening events designed to educate and inspire creatives. Here she gives us an insight into her craft market experiences.

MM: Tell us about your crafting background – have you always made things?

SK: I used to make jewellery when I was at school and even set up a mini-company, selling to classmates and teachers. But professionally, we both have backgrounds in event management: I used to manage events in the charity sector and Stephan used to DJ and run club nights in Dublin. When we moved to London around six years ago, the amazing creativity I saw around me inspired me to rediscover my love of jewellery-making and I created a collection called Galavant. I really enjoyed setting up an Etsy shop, getting to know the handmade community and selling at markets around London. I am currently having a break from Galavant, as I don't have the time to devote to it. Hopefully I will be in a position to pick it up again one day soon.

MM: What made you start Crafty Fox Market?

SK: Back in 2010, I was busy with my fledgling jewellery business, selling at markets around London alongside a day job. We were living in Brixton, South London, but I was often travelling to far-flung parts of the city for events. Sometimes it felt like a gamble whether or not there would be any shoppers there. I decided to start my own event closer to home and poured a lot of energy into promotion. It was only ever intended to be a one-off event, but it was very successful, and as a result vendors wanted to know when the next one would be.

MM: How do you go about organizing it and promoting it – both to other crafters and to the general public?

SK: We started without a network and it was important for us to build trust among the crafting community. For our first event we partnered with Etsy and they helped us to put out the initial call for stallholders. Since then, social media, word of mouth and traditional methods such as posters and flyers have worked well for us. For each event, the talented artist Jimbobart draws a new fox – his work has great appeal and this really helps to create buzz. Strong imagery is often instrumental in helping to gain press coverage for our events.

MM: If you're oversubscribed, how do you go about choosing which stallholders to have?

SK: All of our events have been oversubscribed, so we have been in the fortunate position of being able to select the best stalls from the beginning. We now receive around four applications for every available space and we work with guest curators who bring fresh perspectives each time. We look for unique, quality work that will appeal to our audience.

MM: For a maker selling at a market for the first time, what advice would you give about setting up a successful stall?

SK: Markets are not only a great opportunity to sell but also provide a chance to promote your business. Use the opportunity to build a mailing list and maintain contact with your customers. Place a stack of business cards on your table with the address of your online shop and social media streams. It can also be useful to print out discount codes for free postage to give to potential customers and encourage online sales.

Aim to build height into your display – this creates visual interest and an opportunity to display more products. The aim is to create a cohesive display with a similar look and feel to your online shop. It helps to be well prepared – create a packing list in advance and make sure you know where you are going and how to get there. Take the opportunity to chat to other traders, ask questions and make connections – follow up via social media to maintain links.

At Crafty Fox, we offer new traders an opportunity to be paired up with an experienced trader for advice in advance of the market. Do take advantage of any schemes such as this as they can be great learning experiences.

{ *Top tips* }

Sinead's top tips for crafters who are thinking of organizing a craft market

> Give yourself plenty of time and put a lot of thought into the planning stages. We work with a minimum three-month lead time for each of our events.

> Think about what local organizations you could collaborate with and who could help you to promote the market. While the logistics of any event need to be done properly, the key to success for a craft market is targeted promotion attracting lots of shoppers.

Online marketplaces

There are lots of websites where you can sell your creations, many of them specifically for handmade items. If you're not quite ready to set up your own online store (see page 120), this can be a great way to start.

All these sites have to make money, just as you do, so most of them charge a fee for listing your items as well as another fee once the sale has gone through. Generally, the fees are not exorbitant; you just need to find out in advance what they are so that you can price your goods accordingly and still make a sensible profit. Remember to factor in the fees you will have to pay for PayPal and credit-card payments, too. (For more information on PayPal and credit-card payments, see page 142.)

Only you can decide whether or not a particular site will work for you. Some are very active in marketing and promoting and can give you lots of helpful advice about photographing your products and setting up your online store; others seem to do very little other than guide you through the listings process. Do remember that some sites are so vast that your offerings can easily be swallowed up and difficult for visitors to find, especially if you only have a small number of items for sale. Do check out the sites to see if they're selling lots of items similar to yours. However, you are not locked in to a contract, so it's easy to walk away from them if you find they're not generating enough revenue for you.

Talking to other crafters and joining crafting discussion forums can be useful as well as providing invaluable advice once you're actually selling. Before you sign up, read the small print! Make sure you understand all the terms and conditions – what you're allowed to sell, what the fees are, whether you can sell the same items in other online stores, etc.

eBAY
eBay can be a great place to sell your homemade crafts. All you need to start selling is an eBay account, which can be set up in a matter of minutes. When you're ready to list your first item, go to 'Sell', which you'll find at the top of every eBay page. Then click on 'Sell an item'; the

online form takes you through the whole process, from writing a good title and description to adding photos and setting a price.

When you list an item you pay an insertion fee; when your item sells, you'll also be charged a final value fee, which is a percentage of the total cost to the buyer, including postage, packaging and any other related costs. Insertion and final value fees vary for private and business sellers.

Sellers on eBay.co.uk and eBay.ie have to offer PayPal as a payment method on most listings and in some cases eBay may also require sellers to be PayPal verified for added security. (For payment options in other countries, check the eBay help pages for that country.) You can offer other payment options, including cheque, postal order or credit card (if you have your own processing capabilities), and you can set your payment preferences when you list your item.

ETSY

On Etsy you can only sell handmade goods, 'vintage' items (they have to be at least 20 years old) and crafting supplies. Handmade items must be made by the seller operating the Etsy shop; you cannot list items made by someone else, as that is considered to be reselling.

There are no membership fees on Etsy. Instead you pay a small fee to list each item for four months (or until the item is sold); if it has not sold after four months, the listing expires. You then pay 3.5% of the sales price (excluding shipping costs) when the item is sold.

FOLKSY

Folksy sells handmade items (which you must have made yourself), original designs and crafting supplies. There are two types of account: the basic account, which has no annual membership fee but does entail a small fee for each item listed, and the 'Plus' account, which carries an annual fee (£45 at the time of writing) but no individual listings fees.

NOT ON THE HIGH STREET

In this marketplace you have to apply to be a Partner (currently only available to those with a business address in the UK or Ireland), submit images of your products, and then wait to see if your application has been accepted. If you are accepted, there is a one-off joining fee, but no charge to list your products. Although the joining fee and the commission (around 25%) are high, it still works out less than setting up your own e-commerce business.

Emily Barnes,
Head of Marketing for Folksy.com

Folksy.com is the UK's leading online marketplace for designers and makers to showcase and sell their work. It sells handmade items, original designs and crafting supplies. We asked Head of Marketing Emily Barnes for her top tips on successful online selling.

MM: There are hundreds of shops on Folksy and other online marketplaces. If there's a lot of competition in your chosen field, is there anything you can do to make your shop stand out from the rest?

EB: Yes, lots! First, take great product shots – or invest in a photographer to take them for you. A beautiful, clear image stands out among the others every time. Think about setting your products in a lifestyle shot or using props to show them off at their very best. Second, use keywords in your titles and descriptions to make sure your work is seen by the right people. Mentioning the colour, shape, material or gift occasion (Father's Day, Birthday) can all help potential buyers find your work. Third, hone your craft skills – a quality handmade product will always shine.

MM: How many items should people try to list? If they've only got a very small product range, is it even worth trying – or will their offerings be swamped and hard for customers to find?

EB: We have plenty of successful sellers on Folksy whose collections consist of three or four products in a different colourway. Again, it's about quality not quantity. Your one item, beautifully crafted and photographed, can jump out among 100 other similar products not given the same attention to detail. Folksy also promotes the work of makers through gift guides, home page themes, mail shots and press features so it's ALWAYS worth listing.

MM: What makes a good online shop?

EB: A clear brand image is always the starting point. Before you start to sell, spend some time thinking about what you want your shop to look like. What is it called, what are your ethics? What does it say about you and your work? Develop a clear, unified collection or concept, but be prepared to grow and change as you learn what your customers like. Let your personality shine through and browsers will be drawn in.

MM: What are the benefits of using a site like Folksy to sell your work?

EB: There is no risk when selling on Folksy. You can list your first item for 15p. That's it. No high buy-in costs, no contract, just a beautiful platform for you to get your work seen by hundreds of buyers of handmade. Folksy also allows you to grow by offering advice on selling online and offering services like the Plus Account to those who want to start listing more. We offer secure payment, personalized shop fronts and promotion across our social channels and mail-outs to over 70,000 people. You also get to be part of our amazing community of over 10,000 makers who are there to offer advice, chat to through the messaging service and perhaps indulge in a little mutual buying....

MM: How much help does Folksy give people who are selling for the first time?

EB: We have lots of guidance for first-time sellers. We know it can be daunting, so we've worked hard to make it as simple as simple can be! We have knowledgebase, a service accessed via the Folksy.com home page that holds lots of helpful articles for sellers; a seller blog (blog.folksy.com) with lots and lots of posts to help you get ahead with selling online; and a support team to help those who find they need it. Again, our community offers an amazing source of help and support for everyone from the newest of new sellers to those who have been with us from day one.

Emily on selling online

> Develop a brand: before you start selling online, take the time to think about who you are and who you'd like to appeal to, then go out there and create something stunning.

> Make sure people can find your work: use keywords in product titles and descriptions.

> Have great product photography: if you're not confident about taking your own killer pics, then employ a photographer to do it for you. Think about the types of images that stand out for you and be inspired!

> Immerse yourself in the handmade community. Having a regular 'voice' in the handmade community will do wonders for your sales, so have a go at writing your own craft blog, interact with other bloggers by commenting on their posts, share your new collection ideas across your own social networks and get involved in forum discussions.

> Treat your customers well. You know yourself how lovely it is to get 'happy post', so think about including a hand-written note, use tissue paper or ribbon and always say 'thank you'.

> Look after the figures. Use toolkits like the one offered by mycake.org to help you keep good business habits.

Expert advice from...
Emily Dean, PR & Communications Specialist, Etsy.com

Etsy.com is a marketplace where people around the world connect to buy and sell unique goods. We asked Emily Dean, PR and Communications Specialist, for advice on how to make online marketplaces work for you.

MM: How easy is it for people to list their work on Etsy?

ED: Etsy provides a user-friendly site for sellers to list their items on their shop page. Researching the current market (of your products or items) will help with choosing competitive prices and taking the right photographs (with good lighting, composition and attention to detail) can lead buyers to your shop site. Once you have nailed down your policies (i.e. returns, payment methods), selected your best images and added an enticing description, you're good to go.

MM: How many items should you include in your listing?

ED: Stocking up your shop is incredibly important as items help you get found. The most common way that someone will find your shop is via one of your items. Customers may find an item in a search, or see it featured on Etsy or on a blog. Once they get to an item, they now have access to your shop. The more items you have out there, the more ways you have to be found.

If you don't have much stock it's even more important to use good-quality photographs and if the products are made-to-order or come in different sizes or colours, be sure to mention that. To increase visibility and searchability of your shop's products, your listing titles should start with a list of keywords and phrases that you think your target buyer will search when shopping. Shops will differ in price and stock level. For example, a handmade ceramics shop may have less stock listed than a handmade small accessories shop due to various reasons such as timing and the process in making items. You should list an amount that is realistic to you.

You can also create Treasury Lists that can be published on the Etsy site, attracting buyers and Etsy window shoppers to your shop, through your profile.

MM: Why should people choose to use Etsy?

ED: Etsy is a great site to sell work on because of the support provided – encouraging sellers to build their confidence in themselves and their shop, promote their creativity and ultimately attract more buyers. Etsy also has a worldwide audience, which means you can sell globally from your home.

Etsy also provides:
> Etsy Success newsletter: A twice-weekly email full of tips for growing your shop.
> Teams: Etsy community collectives.

> Online labs: Live and recorded video workshops about selling.
> Help: Find the answers to your Etsy questions with searchable FAQs.
> Seller apps: Tools made by outside developers to help manage your shop.
> Worksheets: Hands-on exercises for developing your shop.

MM: Does Etsy provide help for first-time sellers?

ED: Etsy has a Sellers and Community team that helps first-time sellers. Etsy also has a very detailed Seller Handbook, with step-by-step guides on Setting Up Shop, Product Photography and Shop Graphics, Pricing, Getting Found in Search, Branding & Marketing, Promotion & Media Strategies, Customer Service, Shipping & Packaging, Financing, Legal Info & Inspiration and Motivation.

Emily Dean on how to stand out online

> Good images: Show the value of what you are selling online. Use images that show your work from different angles and possibly illustrate the creative process.

> An enticing description: Describe the item the customer is buying. This might seem obvious, but there are quite a lot of online shops where it just says 'silver vessel'. You need to be as specific as you can; include material, size, weight, manufacturing method, year made and everything that could possibly be of interest to a buyer.

> Make sure you're transparent: Let the customer know exactly how the process works: what happens after they click the button? Do they pay up front or in instalments? How is the money paid, via cheque, bank transfer or credit card? When do you ship the item and how is it handled? What is your returns policy?

> Clear FAQs: If you have questions that customers ask on a regular basis, make sure to include them on your shop profile, as a potential customer probably has the same questions.

> Testimonials: We love to buy something other people have tried and vouched for first, so if you have customer testimonials put them on the site.

Selling from your own website

Even though selling from your own website might seem like a daunting leap, the good news is that, with most ready-made templates, it's really easy to add the pages and links that you'll need.

First, think about how you're going to structure your online store. Obviously, your home page is where you summarize what you're all about. Lots of websites have both a home page and an 'About Us' page, where they can go into more detail about the personalities behind the business and the ethos behind the brand. Think of these as the introductory pages of a traditional printed catalogue. Make sure you strike the right balance between being friendly and accessible and coming across as a professional business.

CATEGORIES AND SUB-CATEGORIES

Then, you need to move on to the products themselves. Start by working out what product categories you need. You might have soft furnishings, clothing and accessories categories, or necklaces, bracelets and earrings. Then think about how you might need to sub-divide those categories; under soft furnishings, for example, you might have sub-categories of curtains and cushions. Remember that you can put products into more than one category if you think it's appropriate – so something like a hand-knitted scarf might be listed under both accessories and gifts. You need to make it as simple as possible for people to find what they're after; try to second guess what headings people would click on to find each item in your product range.

PRODUCT DESCRIPTIONS

Product descriptions are the heart of your online store. In a real shop, customers can see the items on sale, touch them, pick them up, try them on for size. Online, you have to provide all those details.

First, make sure you have a great product shot (see pages 97–103), and that your photos give a really accurate representation of the item. Second is the description itself, the words you use and the information you provide. Keep it factual, not flowery. As always, put yourself in your customers' shoes: if you were buying something similar online, what would you want to know? Remember to include things like size and colour options, care instructions if applicable (machine washable or dry clean only) and, of course, the price.

Some template providers let you add 'If you like this, you may also like these' at the end of a product description, so that you can show similar or related items on your site so customers will be aware of them.

TERMS AND CONDITIONS (T&Cs)

These may actually cover several different pages of your website, but what we're talking about here is all the other information that, by law, you have to give your customers – post and packing information, your returns policy, complaints procedure, contact details. This is covered in more detail on pages 150–151.

There are various ways of working out your shipping costs: it might be by weight, or you might decide to go for a flat fee depending on the total value of the order. Whatever method you choose, remember that you need to take into account not just the postage or courier costs: you also have to work out the cost of packing materials – and it's not at all unreasonable to factor in something for your time if you're going to have to stop work and take parcels to the post office every day.

DATA PROTECTION

Remember that data protection is a factor when customer details are collected, held and processed. The Information Commissioner's Office has lots of information about compliance as well as information on when a company/business will need to be registered on the Data Protection Register. In addition there is a checklist for small businesses that might be a good starting point (www.ico.org.uk).

CHECKOUT

Whether you choose PayPal, credit card payments, or even personal cheques (although these are becoming less popular), the most important thing, of course, is getting paid! These options are discussed on pages 142–143.

Selling to shops

By now, through craft fairs and online sales, you should have built up a good customer base – but to really grow your business, you'll need to expand into other retail outlets.

You might be lucky enough to have shops contact you directly, having seen your work at a trade or craft show or online. More often than not, however, you'll need to make the first approach yourself.

FIRST STEPS

Most makers start locally on a small scale, approaching shops they like and that they feel are a good fit for their brand. One advantage of this can be that people feel a sense of provenance purchasing your products and a real connection to you – something that consumers often feel is worth paying that little bit extra for. It also gives you the chance to become familiar with the whole retailing process and to iron out any glitches in your production system or packaging before you attempt to hit the big time.

So start by looking around your area and drawing up a list of shops to approach. Visit them in person to see the range of products they offer and think carefully about whether your products really are a good fit. Buyers won't thank you for wasting their time trying to persuade them to stock something that is patently unsuitable for their market and customers. But be wary of having your goods in too many competing stores in the same area – although most retailers won't expect exclusivity, they won't want to see exactly the same items on sale in a shop just across the road.

Don't walk in off the street and expect the owner or buyer to see you immediately: he or she may be busy with a customer or have other appointments. Always phone in advance to explain who you are and what you're selling and arrange a convenient time.

Have some samples ready to show – and if your business is making jewellery or clothing, wear it and be your own walking advertisement! Try to exude confidence even if, deep down, you're quaking. Be sure to take a few business cards and a brochure or catalogue – include an order form as well as details of your payment terms and returns policy.

Above all, make sure you have all the facts and figures at your fingertips. Work out your pricing in advance. Will you set a minimum order? Will you give a discount for larger orders? Negotiations can be awkward, but one of the most common mistakes craftspeople make is to undersell themselves, so work out the minimum wholesale price you can accept and do not go below it, no matter how tempting it may be to agree a lower price simply to secure the order.

WHOLESALE AND RETAIL PRICING

We've already looked at the issue of pricing in Chapter 3, but it's so critical that it's worth reiterating a few points here.

First, you need to be absolutely clear about the difference between the wholesale price and the retail price. The retail price is what the customer pays – regardless of whether they're buying direct from you or from a shop. The wholesale price is what a shop pays you; they then add a mark-up to that price in order to cover their own costs and make a profit themselves.

THINKING BIG?

If you're ready to take things to a higher level, enterprise campaign StartUp Britain runs an initiative called PitchUp, which offers emerging British businesses regular opportunities to pitch their products to top buyers. For details, go to www.popupbritain.com and follow the links to PitchUp. Another great event for new designer/makers is the Best of British Design Open Call, which gives successful applicants the opportunity to present their designs directly to the buying panel at London's famous Liberty store and receive some really honest advice about what it takes to be stocked by such a prestigious institution. Check the Liberty website (www.liberty.co.uk) for details of how to register for the current year.

When you're setting your wholesale price, remember that it's made up of four parts: the direct costs of making your product (the raw materials); your time; a percentage of the overheads of running your business; and your profit. If you don't take all of these elements into account, at best you'll scrape a meagre living; at worst, your business could go down the pan in next to no time.

If you're selling to shops for the first time, take a long, hard look at the prices you charge when you sell direct to the public through craft fairs or your own website; if you're dramatically undercutting your stockists and taking sales away from them, they will – understandably – be somewhat peeved.

SALE OR RETURN

Sale or return is an agreement whereby the shop does not pay you up front; instead, you get a percentage of the retail price when your items are sold – typically anything from 40–70%, though it's up to you to negotiate the exact figure. It is more common in smaller shops, which may not have the cash flow to place large or expensive orders. This can make it very hard to manage your own cash flow (see page 144) as you simply don't know when – or even if – the money is likely to come in. However, it does enable you to get your goods into a retail outlet where the general public can see them and, if your business is in its infancy, it can be a great way of getting valuable feedback. As always, you have to weigh up the pros and cons and decide if this option is right for you.

If you do decide to go down this route, make sure you have a proper agreement listing the items you've supplied (including quantities and selling price); how long you've agreed to supply the goods for; who's responsible for insuring the goods while they are on the premises of the retailer; what happens if your items are stolen or damaged while at the shop; how, when and how much you want to be paid for each item; and a statement of ownership, which says that the goods remain yours until you've been paid for them. Ask the shop for references and talk to other crafters to see what their experiences of dealing with that particular shop have been.

Getting shops to stock your goods isn't easy and it can often feel as if you're doing a lot of work for very little return. Don't despair if orders don't come flooding in straight away. It takes a while to build up a reputation and retailers will probably want to test the waters by placing just a small order to begin with. But persevere and you will reap the rewards!

You'll hear lots of financial terms bandied about, so here's a quick jargon buster.

COD
This stands for 'Cash on Delivery', meaning that you won't get paid until you've delivered the goods.

PRO FORMA INVOICE
This is an invoice that you send out for payment for goods prior to their dispatch. It's a good system to use with new customers, until you've established a good working relationship with them and know that they are reliable payers.

EOM
Some retailers (and other customers) will pay their invoices EOM (end of month) – which means that the invoice will be treated as received on the last day of the month in which it was actually received. For example, if you submitted an invoice on 2 January they would treat the invoice as having been received on 31 January – i.e. 28 days later than the actual submission date. This is becoming increasingly popular.

30 DAYS NET
This is the standard for most small-to-medium retailers. It means that you invoice them once you ship the goods and they pay you 30 days from the date of invoice (or from the date they receive the goods, depending on their payment procedures).

60 DAYS NET
Larger retailers may insist on 60 (or even 90) days net; this can have a major impact on your cash flow, so – tempting though it is to agree to it to secure the order – you need to assess whether you can afford to wait that long for payment.

Opening your own shop

Taking on a bricks-and-mortar shop as opposed to an online store can be a scary step, but if you feel ready for the challenge here are some of the things you'll need to consider.

Most makers lease rather than buy a property, giving them the opportunity to try out a location first. Get to know a town or city really well, if you don't already. However, you may not actually need an expensive high-street location: does your business rely on passing trade or will customers come to you, no matter where you are?

Unfortunately, even when you manage to find your dream property, it isn't just a question of giving the place a lick of paint, putting up a few shelves and display units, setting out your gorgeous goods, and waiting for the customers (and money) to roll in. There are lots of legal and financial aspects to take into consideration before you should even contemplate signing on the dotted line. You need to know exactly what you're responsible for and make sure that you factor all the costs in to your business plan and cash flow projections. The checklist below is not definitive and you should take independent professional advice from both a surveyor (to assess the state of the property) and a solicitor or conveyancer (to check out the terms of the lease), but here are some of the things you should think about:

THE BUILDING ITSELF
> Maintenance and repair: Usually the tenant is responsible for this, so it's a good idea to have a proper survey done before you sign the lease, to see what repairs (if any) are needed; if the property is in a poor state of repair, you can then use this as a bargaining tool.
> Does the building meet fire and health and safety regulations? As the tenant, this is your responsibility.
> Does it have disabled access?
> Do the premises have the appropriate planning classification for your business? Most shops fall within Class A1 (retail), but if you're intending to include a café in your shop and sell food and drink for

consumption on the premises, you'll need Class A3. There would also be legal requirements relating to the sale of food and drink, as well as possible licensing obligations in terms of food standards and health and safety. And in the event that music is played in a shop, you would need a licence to play music from the PPL (in the UK).

> Who is responsible for insuring the building and its contents?

COSTS AND CHARGES

> How much is the rent and when will it be reviewed? Most shop leases are for 10 years and include rent reviews at periodic intervals.
> Is the rent due weekly, monthly or quarterly? In arrears or advance?
> How much are the business rates? Each property has a rateable value (RV). The government then levies a Uniform Business Rate (UBR), which is revised annually. You can find out the rateable value of the property from your local council.
> Do you need to pay a deposit?
> Are utilities bills (water, gas, electricity, phone line) included in the rent?
> Could you negotiate a rent-free period in order to do any necessary renovations and fit out the shop?

LEASE DURATION AND RENEWAL

> Is this a new lease or are you taking over an existing lease? If it's an existing lease, how long is left to run?
> Is there an early get-out option?
> Do you have the right to reassign the lease to someone else should your business plans change in the future?
> Are you allowed to sub-let any of the space?

Opening a shop certainly isn't something to be undertaken lightly. But in the current economic climate, with so many commercial properties standing empty, there's definitely the opportunity to negotiate.

POP-UP SHOPS

These are shops that are in business for just a short space of time, giving you the perfect opportunity to test products and locations without committing to a long-term lease. To find out more, go to www.appearhere.co.uk, www.popupbritain.com, www.popupspace.com or www.wearepopup.com.

Running workshops

You may not realize it, but as a craftsperson you have one advantage over many new businesses: not only can you sell the things you create, but you can also sell your expertise by running workshops and imparting your knowledge to others.

This can be a really lucrative extra revenue stream, and a good way of covering some of the cost of renting your studio space or shop – particularly during the evenings or at weekends when the space would not normally be used. If you don't have a separate studio or shop, why not look into hiring a room at your local community centre for an afternoon or evening? Alternatively, approach local arts centres and schools – anywhere that runs evening or weekend classes for the community – and see if they might be interested in hiring space to you or taking you on as a tutor.

Don't worry if you have no prior experience: you're going to be teaching something you're passionate about, which is a great start. And your students will be keen to learn everything they can, so it's not like facing a classroom full of bored kids who can't wait for lessons to be over for the day. It's still a bit daunting, though – after all, people are handing over their hard-earned cash for your pearls of wisdom and a few negative comments on Facebook can be quite damaging. So what can you do to make your workshops a success?

FIRST STEPS
First, find out if there really is a market for what you're offering. If you're at a craft fair or have an email newsletter or blog, use it as a way of finding out what subjects people are interested in and whether a beginners, intermediate or advanced workshop would attract the most students. Do some research into what other people are charging for their workshops and what they offer their students, too.

Once you've decided to give it a go, promote your workshops in any way you can – put up posters in your shop or studio window, distribute leaflets locally, put a flyer in with every purchase when you're selling at your local craft fair, use social media and do everything you can to get the word out there.

Make sure you've got the right insurance in place: public liability insurance is a must, but you might also want to consider taking out professional indemnity insurance (see page 149).

RUN A TRIAL WORKSHOP FOR FAMILY AND FRIENDS

This will give you the chance to sort out all kinds of practicalities: how far in advance you ask for payment, how much pre-course information you send out, how long it's going to take you to set up, exactly what you're going to demonstrate, whether your explanations are clear enough for beginners, how much you can realistically cover in the time, what equipment and materials you need, how many students you can cope with at one time, the kind of questions they're likely to ask, and so on. It's far better to make your initial mistakes in front of a group of friends and family than in front of paying strangers.

KNOW YOUR CUSTOMER

It's tempting to try to make your workshops appeal to as many people as you can. We've all seen adverts claiming that a class is 'for all ages from 9 to 90' or 'suitable for beginners and experienced crafters' – but put yourself in your customers' shoes for a moment. If you were a complete beginner, wouldn't you feel a bit frustrated being in the same workshop as someone who's forging ahead while you're still struggling with the basics – and vice versa? So target your workshops at a specific skill level: you'll still get some people who work faster than others and some who demand more of your time than others, but the overall balance will be better for everyone.

OFFER INCENTIVES

Is there anything extra you can offer that will encourage people to sign up? A discount for booking early or on materials that they buy from you on the day, perhaps? A glass of wine at lunchtime or at the end of the workshop? Perhaps you could offer a special price for a group booking for a group of friends or work colleagues?

BOOKING PROCEDURES

When people sign up, follow up immediately by sending them a booking confirmation along with any other information they might need. It's a good idea to include a basic timetable at this point – for example:

9.45 a.m.	Arrive
10.00	Demonstration
10.15–11.15	Students' work time
11.15–11.30	Coffee break
11.30–11.45	Demonstration
11.45-1.00	Students' work time
1.00–2.00	Lunch

This will not only show students that you've planned everything carefully, but it will also give you a time framework to work to, so you will know if your demonstration is over-running and you're not leaving enough time for people to try things out for themselves.

Also be sure to include details of anything the students need to bring, along with directions on how to find the venue and parking instructions if they're bringing their own cars. If you're providing lunch (see below), this is the time to ask if people have any food allergies or special dietary requirements.

BE PREPARED

Preparation is everything – and it always takes longer than you think. Plan the session carefully, bearing in mind that you have to allow time to demonstrate as well as for the students to work on their own creations. Think about how best to arrange your workshop space. Decide on a maximum and a minimum class size: running a workshop for just one or two people probably won't be financially viable, but having too many students will mean you won't be able to give them all the individual attention they need. Source all the equipment and materials you need well in advance. If you want the students to bring things themselves – even if it's just a notebook and pen – send out a list with each booking confirmation. If you're providing food, get it ready in advance or arrange to have it brought into the workshop at a specified time. On the day, get there in plenty of time; you don't want to be setting things up when the first students arrive! In fact, if you can set everything up the evening before, so much the better.

CREATE THE RIGHT ATMOSPHERE

Keep things relaxed and friendly – you're running a hands-on workshop, not delivering a formal lecture. Encourage the participants to interact and ask questions. To break the ice, maybe you could start by asking everyone to introduce themselves and explain what made them sign up for the workshop and what they're hoping to take away from it; that will also give you a chance to assess people's level of skill and their expectations of you.

INVITING OTHER CRAFTERS

At some point, you might also want to think about inviting other crafters to give workshops in your studio. Obviously you'd have to give them a share of the fees, so it's not as profitable as running the whole thing yourself, but if your workshop space is underused it's worth considering. You'd also need to be very clear about who was doing what – for example, who would promote the workshop and be responsible for taking bookings, who would set up the space and provide the materials and so on. If another crafter gave a badly run workshop, it would reflect badly on you, as the organizer, so make sure you're confident in their abilities and organizational skills as well as in your own. And it's probably a good idea if their subject area complements your own, so that there's some obvious link with the kind of products and course you offer.

See also:
Using social media, page 80
Insurance, page 148

The customer is king

Whether you've got a stall at a craft fair, an online presence or an actual shop front, it is essential that you treat each customer as you'd like to be treated yourself.

It sounds basic, but you would be amazed at the number of people who don't even look up when you enter their store. The customer service that you provide is every bit as important as your products – so make 'service with a smile' your mantra. Every customer wants to feel valued and every customer has the potential to introduce new people to your business and make it a success. We think of it like this:

tells friends about your shop

gives gift to designated recipient

recipient delighted with gift and asks where it's from

recipient's friends see gift and ask where it's from

one or all of those people come to your shop

customer buys gift

Once you've got your customers, you want to keep them. There are a number of ways you can do this, but here are just some of our suggestions:

Be interested in them and ask if there's anything else they are looking for – but be aware that some people may just want to browse and may feel they're being pressured into buying if you're too chatty or pushy. You have to be able to recognize when you need to back off.

Get to know regular customers by name and remember details about them. Invite them to shopping evenings and offer incentives such as a glass of wine or a discount.

Set up an email newsletter and ask people if they'd like to be included on it. This way, they'll know instantly when you're launching a new product or service or hosting a special event. Try something like Mailchimp (www.mailchimp.com) or Constant Contact (www.constantcontact.com) for an easy-to-use template.

Make sure you update your blog regularly (see page 80).

Consider loyalty schemes. Many coffee shops, for example, have cards that are stamped each time a customer buys a coffee and they then get the eleventh one free. Could you do something similar – perhaps stamping a card every time they buy goods over a certain value and then giving either a discount or a free gift when they've clocked up five or ten stamps?

Last but not least, never make a promise you can't keep. If you know that a certain line is out of stock or that you can't guarantee delivery in the timeframe they want, for example, be honest about it. They'll appreciate your candour – but let them down and you'll lose their trust.

DEALING WITH COMPLAINTS

It's no secret that 'the customer is always right', but it is not always easy to handle complaints or criticism, especially at the start of your new venture. Do not be put off. Should you receive a disgruntled email, angry phone call or even have a face-to-face encounter, be patient and listen to what they have to say.

Acknowledge the complaint as soon as you are able – ideally within 24 hours – and let them know the matter is in hand. If you're going to be away at a craft fair for a few days, set up an auto reply on your email. Don't be tempted to engage in any argument, however much you believe them to be wrong. Respond quickly, politely and efficiently, so they can see you're taking the complaint seriously, and they'll be much more likely to forgive you for any faulty goods or small mistake that might have occurred. Ignoring it in the hope that the problem will just go away is a recipe for disaster; with social media, bad publicity can spread like wildfire, and one angry customer can easily make a fledgling business pay the price.

See also:

Consumer law in brief, page 150

Chapter 6

The nitty gritty

Money, money, money...

It goes without saying that good accounting is absolutely essential for every business, yet lots of craftspeople freely admit they're not good with figures. We can't turn you into a professional accountant with one wave of a magic wand, but here are some of the things you should consider.

HIRING A BOOKKEEPER OR ACCOUNTANT

You may well be able to do all your bookkeeping yourself, particularly in the early stages of your business, but why not consider hiring someone to come in once or twice a month?

A bookkeeper can handle all the day-to-day financial tasks, submitting invoices promptly and chasing up payment, paying the bills, keeping track of expenses and making sure that every cost has been entered correctly into whatever accounting software you're using. They'll probably do the job much more quickly and efficiently than you would and you'll be able to devote the time you've saved to other aspects of your business.

An accountant will analyze your overall financial situation and can give you more of a strategic overview. He or she will also produce key financial documents such as a profit-and-loss statement, if needed, and file your tax returns. Again, if you're a sole trader and your business finances are relatively straightforward, you could do all this yourself – if you have the time and the inclination. However, financial regulations and tax thresholds change from year to year; qualified accountants not only make a point of keeping up to date, but they'll know exactly what you can and cannot claim as legitimate business expenses, whereas it might take you a while to figure it all out yourself – and you can offset their fees against your tax liability, too.

But if you do decide to hire in help, don't abnegate all responsibility: this is YOUR business and you need to be fully conversant with its finances, even if you're not actually filling in all those spreadsheets and forms yourself. And you can make your bookkeeper or accountant's life much easier (and probably save yourself money in the process) by keeping all your financial records in good order. Storing receipts and invoices in an old shoebox is all very well, but even for an experienced professional it can be a nightmare trying to make sense of everything – especially if you leave it until just before your tax return is due!

CHOOSING AN ACCOUNTANT

In the UK, make sure that your accountant has qualified through one of the main accountancy bodies such as the Chartered Institute of Management Accountants (CIMA), the Institute of Chartered Accountants (either ICAEW or ICAS) or the Association of Chartered Certified Accountants (ACCA). These bodies hold their members to account in the event of bad practice, so you'll be afforded some protection if things go wrong.

In the USA you will want to ensure that your accountant is a Certified Public Accountant (CPA). For more information visit www.cpadirectory.com.

SETTING UP A BUSINESS BANKING ACCOUNT

If you are setting up a business as a sole trader, limited company or partnership, there is no legal requirement to have a business banking account, although keeping your personal and business accounts separate can make it easier to manage your business finances.

There are many different types of account to choose from, each with different features. Do your research rather than just setting up another account with the bank you've always used for your personal finances, as you may well get a better deal elsewhere.

Check the small print for charges. Is there a monthly fee? What's the overdraft rate? Will your bank charge you for depositing cash? If you think you will mainly be making payments electronically, go for an account that offers free or low-cost electronic transactions. Alternatively, if you think you'll be using a lot of cheques, look for low charges on paper transactions. Many accounts give you free banking for the first 12 or 18 months, but find out what rates will apply after that period. Some banks have branch-based business advisers, as well as offering advice over the phone or online, and this can be invaluable.

With so many banks competing for your custom, it can be hard to decide which is offering the best deal. Start by consulting a comparison website to see what different accounts offer, then make an appointment with the bank in question to find out more.

CHOOSING ACCOUNTING SOFTWARE THAT WORKS FOR YOU

Gone are the days when 'keeping the books' involved bespectacled clerks meticulously entering figures by hand in a leather-bound ledger; in today's digital age, there's a bewildering array of accounting software available, all of it claiming to make managing your business finances a doddle. So how do you choose?

The first question to ask yourself is what bookkeeping tasks you actually need it to perform – for example, budgeting; stock control; invoicing and receipts; purchases and payments; banking and cash management; VAT, tax and accounts; payroll. If you trade overseas, can the software handle different currencies? How easy is it to import and export information from other programs (word-processing programs or spreadsheets, for example) or to add new fields?

Some accounting packages have been developed specifically for small businesses; these include Sage Instant Accounts and Sage 50, Intuit QuickBooks SimpleStart and QuickBooks Pro, and Microsoft Money Plus Home & Business. More advanced accounting packages come in modules, with each module handling one aspect of financial management (for example, sales ledger) – for example, Sage 200 and Pegasus Opera. When you've narrowed down your options, find out if the software you're thinking of buying will be able to grow with your business. Will you be able to add modules later – for example, payroll if your business grows to the point where you need to employ other people?

Does the software come with a free trial? It's always best if you can try before you buy.

Make sure that your existing computer hardware can run the software you're thinking of buying, as having to upgrade your entire IT system is going to be costly.

Talk to your accountant before you take the plunge, as he or she may be able to recommend software that works with programs they have. Some accountants may help you set up your accounting software so that it gathers the data they need to help you file your taxes, as well. Find out what businesses similar to yours are using; this is where business networking (see page 47) can really help you. And check out online reviews on the newest progams.

Above all, take your time over this decision: you don't want to have to scrap your entire accounting system a few years down the line if you find that your business has outgrown it.

FIND OUT MORE

For more information on accounting software, go to:

> www.intuit.co.uk/QuickBooks
> www.microsoft.com
> www.pegasus.co.uk
> www.sage.co.uk

Tax

To quote Benjamin Franklin, 'Only two things are certain in this world: death and taxes.' There's no way of knowing when the grim reaper will come knocking at your door, but the taxman comes calling with relentless regularity – so be prepared.

Sole traders and partnerships must register for self-assessment with HMRC as soon as possible after starting their business and file an annual self-assessment tax return, which is used to work out the amount of income tax and national insurance payments that are due. The deadline for filing your annual tax return is 31 October for a paper return or 31 January if you are filing online; there are financial penalties for sending your tax return in late, so don't leave it to the last minute. File early and you will know well in advance exactly what income tax and national insurance contributions you have to pay. Even better, get into the habit of putting a proportion of your income aside in a separate account each month, so that the money for your tax bill is there when you need it.

You can deduct many of the costs and expenses associated with running your business from your income to work out your taxable profit. Expenses allowed by HMRC include stationery, phone and Internet costs, postage, business travel costs, business banking, PayPal and credit-card charges, raw materials, accountancy and other professional fees, and a proportion of your rent, rates, power and water if you work from home – but not, contrary to popular belief, long boozy lunches entertaining prospective customers. You may also be able to get 'capital allowances' on certain other costs, such as specialist machinery that you need to make your products, which will also reduce your taxable profits. Your accountant will be able to tell you what is allowed.

There are two deadlines for paying any tax that is due: 31 January for paying anything due for the previous tax year and for making your first payment on account towards the current year's tax bill; and 31 July for making your second payment on account. As with filing your tax return, there are financial penalties for late payment. You should keep financial records for five years after the online tax return deadline.

Limited companies must register for corporation tax within three months of starting to trade as a business. You must normally file your company tax return within 12 months of the end of your company's corporation tax accounting period. Unlike income tax self-assessment, where the dates for filing returns and making payments are usually the same, the deadline for paying corporation tax is *before* the deadline for filing your company tax return.

Tax is a complex subject and there isn't space here to give anything more than a very brief overview; moreover, tax thresholds and legislation change from year to year, so – unless your tax affairs are incredibly straightforward – seek professional advice.

VALUE ADDED TAX (VAT)

VAT is not something that most new businesses have to worry about, as you don't have to register unless your turnover for the previous 12 months has gone over a specific limit or you think it will soon exceed this limit. If your business is VAT registered, you must charge VAT on the goods and services you provide; however, you can reclaim the VAT you pay when you buy goods and services for your business. (If you're not VAT registered, then you can't reclaim VAT that you've paid.)

You can also register voluntarily for VAT. Although volunteering to pay extra tax might sound like a crazy thing to do, there may be cash-flow advantages in being able to charge VAT on your sales and claim it back on your purchases; however, as VAT on most sales in the UK is charged at 20%, you will have to put your prices up to maintain the same profit margin. If you charge customers for delivery and packing, you will probably have to charge VAT on those costs as well as on the item you've sold. Seek advice from your accountant.

FIND OUT MORE
> In the UK go to www.hmrc.gov.uk
> In the USA visit www.irs.gov

Card and online payments

If your business is going to grow, at some point you will have to get to grips with debit and credit card payments and with the intricacies of accepting payment online.

ACCEPTING CARD PAYMENTS

To process credit or debit card payments, you need to have an account with the merchant services department of a bank. This is different to a business bank account: it is where your customers' card details are securely sent for authorization. There are different types of merchant accounts, depending on whether you want to accept card payments online or by telephone or mail order, or do repeat billing. Most leading banks offer merchant services; shop around for the best deal.

The application process is strict and not every business is accepted. Once you have been accepted, you will have to rent a card terminal, usually for a monthly fee. When you make a sale, the terminal sends details of each transaction to the bank, which will settle with the customer's card issuer. Within three to four days it will credit your business with the amount, minus an authorization fee for each transaction. The fee can be anything from 1.5 to 5% of the transaction value and may be different for debit and credit cards.

To take card payments online you will need an Internet Merchant Account (IMA) as well as a payment gateway service to move the money securely between your website's shopping cart and the banks or credit card companies involved with the transactions. You can apply for an IMA from a traditional high-street bank or from Payment Service Providers (PSPs) such as PayPal or Sage Pay, which can give you an IMA and payment gateway in one package.

ONLINE PAYMENT SERVICE PROVIDERS (PSPS)

There are lots of PSPs out there and there isn't space here to do more than take a very brief look at two of the best known – but do shop around. When choosing, find out about their rates, any upfront costs, what technical support they provide, and what kind of fraud protection they offer.

PayPal

PayPal is the biggest and probably the most popular online payment service provider. Buyers can send payments free of charge from their computer or web-enabled phone and pay using either their own PayPal account or (if you're set up to receive card payments) most major credit and debit cards. When the order is complete, the money usually shows up in your PayPal account in a few minutes.

For sellers, there is a flat fee of 3.4% plus (at the time of writing) 20p per transaction, If you've received more than £1,500 in PayPal payments in the previous calendar month, you can apply for discounted 'merchant rates' – so the more you sell, the less you pay.

For business users, PayPal offers Standard and Pro accounts. The Standard account has no set-up fee, no monthly fees and no cancellation charge. For start-up and small online businesses, this is a good option. The Pro account does have a monthly fee, but it allows you to host checkout directly on your own website (with the standard account, customers are taken to the payment pages on the PayPal site) and to accept card payments by phone and mail order. The Pro account is more suitable for larger, established businesses.

There is also a relatively new development called PayPal Here™, a Chip & Pin device that you might find useful for craft fairs where customers may run out of ready cash and not have access to an ATM. You pay a one-off fee for the reader, plus a transaction fee (which varies depending on how the customer is paying).

Sage Pay

With Sage Pay, there are no set-up fees, percentage fees or annual charges; for the standard package you pay a monthly fee, which entitles you to 1,000 online or phone transactions per quarter for a monthly fee; above 1,000 transactions per month, you pay a small fixed fee per transaction instead. Sage Pay Go enables you to accept card payments online, over the phone or via mail order. It also includes 24-hour telephone and email support and fraud screening and prevention tools.

FIND OUT MORE
www.paypal.com/uk
www.sagepay.com

Managing your cash flow

More often than not, the biggest problem facing any new business is not a lack of marketable ideas or being unable to get hold of the right supplies: it's cash flow. Even if you're employing someone else to do your bookkeeping, as the owner you have to understand how cash flow affects your business.

To put it simply, cash flow is the difference between the amount of money coming in to your business during a given period and the amount of money going out. To manage your cash flow, you need to know not just *how much* money you've got coming in and going out, but also *when* those payments will be made.

Say that, over the course of one month, you spent £500 on raw materials and £1,000 on labour costs and overheads and you sold goods to the value of £2,500. You sold £1,000 more than you spent, so there's no problem – right? Not necessarily! If you sold those goods for cash at craft fairs or in your own shop, you've got the money in your hot, sticky little hands. But if you agreed payment terms of 90 days net with a major retailer, you won't get paid for three whole months after you delivered the goods. And if you have to wait that long, do you have enough in the bank to buy more materials, pay all your bills, and pay yourself and any staff a living wage in the meantime?

This is why doing a cash-flow forecast is so important. You need to look ahead and be pro-active (forestalling problems before they happen) rather than reactive (dealing with problems when they arise). But once you've done one, don't just tick it off your 'to do' list and leave it languishing on your computer: you have to review it and update it regularly, so that you're completely on top of your finances at all times.

The best way to do a cash-flow forecast is to use a spreadsheet such as Excel or another software program recommended by your accountant or bookkeeper, setting out your monthly receipts and outgoings. The individual entries will vary depending on the exact nature of your business, but below is a sample of the kinds of things you should include. It's not rocket science, but there are a few things that can catch you out if you're not careful. For example, 'Sales – credit' does not mean credit-card sales, which are treated as cash – it refers to sales where you invoice and give the buyer a period of credit (30, 60 or even 90) days; although they pay in 30 days it will be 35–40 days before the money has actually cleared through to your account, so you need to put those figures in the month in which you will receive payment, not in the month in which you invoice. Again, your accountant or bookkeeper will be able to advise you on this.

IDEAS FOR IMPROVING YOUR CASH FLOW

> Offer discounts to customers who pay their bills promptly.
> Run a credit check on all new non-cash customers to see if they're likely to be reliable payers.
> Get rid of old stock for whatever you can get.
> Send out invoices promptly.
> Chase overdue invoices immediately.
> Negotiate with your own suppliers – get the best payment terms you can from them and if a payment is due in 30 days, don't pay it in 15 days.
> Finally, if you do happen to run into difficulties, don't bury your head in the sand. Be honest with both your suppliers and your bank.

Expert advice from...

Patricia van den Akker, Director of The Design Trust

The Design Trust (www.thedesigntrust.co.uk) is an online business school for people who want to start, run and grow their own design or craft business. Patricia van den Akker has been an adviser, coach, trainer and mentor for nearly 15 years. Here she shares her advice for keeping on top of your finances.

MM: Good bookkeeping is essential for any business. What's the best way to keep track of your incomings and outgoings?

PvdA: Have a practical system in place, and allocate enough time to do your finances. Keep all your receipts, invoices and bank statements in a folder. Depending on your income and expenditure, you will have to spend a couple of hours on your accounts on a regular basis. Don't let it pile up, as your finances will soon get out of control.

I think it is really useful to allocate, for example, the first and third Monday of every month to doing your accounts. Note it down in your diary as your 'financial meeting'. Making physical time in your diary will help you to actually do it.

On your finance day, start with your income: create your invoices and send them, record them, update income records, and contact late payers. Then do your expenses: file the incoming invoices, pay your suppliers, record payments, update your records.

Most importantly, update your cash-flow forecast for the next weeks. Cash flow is crucial for new businesses, because if you run out of money then you won't have a business. This is especially a problem if you create products and you have to pay for raw materials and your overheads often weeks or months before you will get paid yourself. Always keep an eye on your bank balance, and forecast how much money will be coming in that month and how much will go out.

MM: What are the biggest financial challenges most new businesses face?

PvdA: I think there are three: lack of money, money management/cash flow, and undervaluing your work.

Businesses often don't realize how much money they need to start their business. Or they might have just enough money to get started, but then run out of money to keep going. Often businesses generate very little money in the first three years or so, and you will need money to invest in your business. The amount of money you can pay to yourself as a salary will often be very low. Very often people start a business while doing a full-time or part-time job elsewhere, just to make sure that they can pay their own personal bills.

Second, many creative start-ups do not plan ahead for their business. It is important to know what your start-up costs will be, and to forecast your income and expenditure for the first year. Also do a cash-flow forecast.

But more important is that you review these financials regularly (at least once a month) and come up with a plan of action if the reality isn't in line with your expectations.

Third, many creatives start their business as a hobby. But running a successful business long term means that you need to be aware of your real costs (including your time and overheads), and you need to calculate them properly and charge accordingly. Don't undervalue your products if you want to succeed long term.

MM: Sorting out their tax and VAT returns fills most people with dread. How do you get everything done efficiently?

PvdA: Keep on top of your finances by updating your finances regularly. Have a system that you understand, and keep all the info together so that it is easy to find what is going on. File online instead of by paper, as the computer will calculate automatically how much you owe HMRC. Plus the deadline for filing is later.

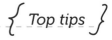
{ Top tips }

Patricia on keeping on top of your finances

> Have a filing system that works for you, so that you always have all the info together and don't need to start looking for lost invoices – even if that is just a box where everything goes until you have the time to do your accounts.

> Get an overdraft when you are still in credit. An overdraft is a great way to help you with any small cash-flow fluctuations. A bank is far more likely to offer you an overdraft facility when you are in credit than when you are already in debt.

> Don't use credit cards – this is a very expensive way to pay for regular business costs or to bridge any financial gaps.

> Schedule regular meetings with your accountant or bookkeeper. You are more likely to update your accounts before your meeting with them, and they can discuss your financial situation with you.

> Don't close your eyes if you are running into trouble. Talk to somebody to help you sort your finances out and get back in control.

Insurance

Unless you work in the insurance industry, it's unlikely that you'll find the thought of insurance very exciting. Exciting it may not be, but essential it is.

Imagine someone came to your shop, tripped and fell over, injuring themselves and damaging your stock. First, there's the risk they might try to sue you; second, your stock might be lost for ever. Or what if there was a flood or a fire? Protect yourself and your business by making sure you have the right kinds of insurance in place.

BUILDINGS AND CONTENTS INSURANCE

If you're renting or leasing your business property, you need to check what your landlord's insurance covers; it's likely to be just the building itself, so you will need comprehensive contents insurance. If you're working from home, having buildings insurance will already be a condition of your mortgage, but you will need to make sure your contents insurance covers all your business equipment and stock. However, some materials and equipment (kilns, for example) may be excluded from your normal domestic cover, so check with your insurance provider. If you do need to make a claim and you haven't told them everything, your claim may be invalid.

PUBLIC LIABILITY INSURANCE

Public liability insurance protects against claims brought against a business by other people. It provides cover for any injury to any other person or damage to property while you are going about your business activities. It can also cover products supplied by you and your business. If someone tripped over something that you'd left lying around at a craft fair, for example, they might decide to pursue a claim against you rather than the fair organizers. Some craft fairs insist that you have your own public liability insurance. If you take out this insurance, make sure that it covers you for both indoor and outdoor craft fairs; also be sure to check that you have the right level of cover.

PRODUCT LIABILITY INSURANCE

This gives you cover in the event of a claim for damage or injury arising from defects in your product – for example, if the eyes on a toy bunny weren't sewn on securely and a child swallowed and choked on one.

PROFESSIONAL INDEMNITY INSURANCE

If you're running workshops or writing tutorials on aspects of your craft, this is something you might wish to consider. It will give you cover in the event of someone making a claim against you for negligent advice.

CRITICAL ILLNESS INSURANCE

If you fall ill with certain critical illnesses or become permanently disabled as a result of injury or illness, this type of insurance covers you by paying out a tax-free lump sum.

BUSINESS INTERRUPTION INSURANCE

This will cover you against loss of earnings if you have to spend time replenishing your stock following theft, fire and so on.

EMPLOYER LIABILITY INSURANCE

Employer liability insurance covers a business if any of its employees have an accident at work and are making a claim against the business. It is a legal requirement to hold employer liability insurance if: you are not a limited company but have staff (i.e. people who work for you excluding business partners or family members). These include any persons working under your guidance and using your tools and equipment; if you are a limited company with more than one person; if you are a limited company consisting only of yourself, and manual and clerical staff, but own less than 51% of the business.

OTHER TYPES OF INSURANCE

The types of insurance listed above are probably the most important, but there are other types of insurance that you might want to consider. These include: exhibition cover, where you can insure against losses due to the cancellation or postponement of fairs and trade shows; and trade credit insurance cover if you have a placed a lot of stock with retailers on a sale or return basis (see page 124) and the stockist goes out of business.

Consumer law in brief

There are a number of pieces of legislation that cover the sale of goods and services to members of the public. These set out the stipulations that cover both the manner in which products/ services are sold and also the products themselves.

The key ones are: Sale of Goods Act; Supply of Goods and Services Act; Unfair Terms in Consumer Contracts; Distance Selling Regulations; Electronic Commerce Regulations; and Consumer Protection from Unfair Trading Regulations. Before you sell to the public, make sure you are aware of the implications of this legislation.

SALE OF GOODS ACT 1979

For retailers in the UK, this Act states that goods must be 'as described, of satisfactory quality and fit for purpose'. 'As described' means that the goods sold must match any description that the consumer saw – either in a shop or in a printed brochure or catalogue. 'Fit for purpose' means the goods must be able to do what they were designed to do; for example, a necklace should have a clasp that fastens and stays fastened. If goods don't meet these criteria, then the buyer may have a claim against the retailer – that is, you. All businesses that supply goods, including online and distance sellers, must follow the Sale of Goods Act.

How does this affect you?

If the item you've sold is faulty, the customer can ask for a repair, refund or replacement – but this must be done within a 'reasonable' amount of time. What's 'reasonable' depends on the product and how obvious the fault is. (This would prevent someone from using something for a year and then claiming it was faulty if it broke due to normal wear and tear.)

Customers do not have a legal right to a refund, repair or replacement because of normal wear and tear or if they simply change their mind. And if an item is personalized – a bib embroidered with the baby's name, for example – the customer cannot return it (unless it is faulty).

DISTANCE SELLING REGULATIONS (DSRs)

In addition to the protection offered by the Sale of Goods Act, these protect the rights of customers buying at a distance – for example, online or over the phone – where they cannot meet the supplier face to face and inspect the goods or services offered for sale.

'Pre-contract' information

Before customers order from you, you must provide 'pre-contract' information. This must include a description of the goods or services; clear, legible pricing; whether delivery costs are included; how payment can be made; your full trading address (even if it is your home address) and contact details; your VAT number, if you have one; the timeframe within which the goods will be delivered; and information about your customers' rights to cancel the order.

Information you must give once your customer has ordered

You must also provide pre-contract information in writing or other form that cannot be edited (e.g. fax or email). You should also tell customers how to exercise their right to cancel, who will pay for returns, details of any guarantees or after-sales services, and how to make a complaint. You must acknowledge receipt of orders electronically as soon as possible and take reasonable steps to allow customers to correct errors in their order. Finally, ensure your T&Cs can be downloaded and printed.

Cancellation and returns

Customers can cancel an order from the moment it is placed to seven working days (not including weekends or bank holidays) after they receive the goods. If they want to cancel, they must tell you in writing or in another medium such as email – but they cannot do so by phone, unless your terms say this is acceptable. The customer must pay for the cost of returning the goods only if this is covered in the contract and information provided. However, if the goods are faulty or you substitute items that the customer doesn't want, you must pay the return costs.

OTHER CONSUMER LEGISLATION

Under the Consumer Protection from Unfair Trading Regulations there are 31 specific practices that are banned as unfair commercial practices. Electronic Commerce Regulations exist to ensure that online contracts are legally binding and enforceable throughout Europe.

Employing staff

Most creative businesses start off with just one person, or perhaps two people working in partnership, but as your business grows you may need extra help. If you're employing staff for the first time, there are some things that you are required by law to do.

REGISTER AS AN EMPLOYER

If you are paying staff at or above the PAYE threshold, at or above the National Insurance Lower Earnings limit, or providing employee benefits, you must inform HM Revenue and Customs (HMRC) and enrol for PAYE. You can do this up to four weeks before you pay your staff. All employers have to give details of their name, business name, contact details and the date of their first payday or employee benefits. Once you are registered, HMRC will provide your PAYE and Accounts Office references.

TAKE OUT EMPLOYERS' LIABILITY INSURANCE

As soon as you become an employer, you will normally need employers' liability insurance up to the value of at least £5 million; you may not need it if you only employ a family member or someone who is based abroad, but be sure to check with your insurance broker or provider. Employers' liability insurance will help you meet the costs of damages and legal fees for employees who are injured or made ill through the work they do for you. Your insurer must be authorized and you must display your certificate of insurance at your workplace.

CHECK YOUR EMPLOYEES ARE ELIGIBLE TO WORK IN THE UK

Make sure that anyone you employ has the legal right to work in the UK – you can be prosecuted and fined if you employ illegal workers.

DECIDE HOW MUCH YOU'RE GOING TO PAY THEM

You must pay at least the national minimum wage; this applies to part-time workers as well as full-time. If you're taking on an apprentice, then he or she will get an apprentice rate if under 19 or in their first year.

PROVIDE A WRITTEN STATEMENT OF EMPLOYMENT

If you're employing someone for more than one month, you must give them a written statement of employment within two months of them starting work, setting out the business's name; the employee's name, job title or a description of work and start date; how much and how often the employee will get paid; hours of work and whether Sunday, night or overtime working is required; details of holiday entitlement and whether or not that includes public holidays – almost all workers are entitled to 28 days' paid holiday per year (*pro rata* for part-time workers); where the employee will be working and whether they might have to relocate if you moved the location of your business; if an employee works in different places, where these will be and what the employer's address is. It must also contain information about duration of contracts; notice periods; pensions; complaints and grievance procedures; sick pay; and disciplinary and dismissal procedures.

HEALTH AND SAFETY

Under the Health and Safety at Work Act 1974, you have a duty of care to ensure that your employees are safe at work. You must complete a risk assessment and health and safety arrangements must be up to date.

FIND OUT MORE

> See if your insurer is authorized to provide employers' liability insurance at www.fca.org.uk.
> To register with HMRC as an employer, go to www.hmrc.gov.uk.
> To check if someone can work in the UK, go to www.gov.uk/legal-right-to-work-in-the-uk.
> For information on the national minimum wage, go to www.gov.uk/national-minimum-wage.
> In the USA the US Department of Labor will provide the information you need; www.dol.gov.

Resources

Here is a list of contacts and links that you may find useful when setting up your business – in whatever form.

BUILDING YOUR 'BRAND'
www.companieshouse.gov.uk; +44 (0)303 1234 500
www.businesslink.gov.uk
www.ccoi.ie; +353 (0)56 7761804
www.designcouncil.org.uk; +44 (0)207 420 5200
www.crowdspring.com; 001 877 887 7442
www.sba.gov; 001 800 827 5722

YOUR COMPANY STRUCTURE
www.gov.uk
www.companieshouse.gov.uk; +44 (0)303 1234 500
www.hmrc.gov.uk
www.sba.gov.uk, 001 800 827 5722

HOME OR AWAY?
www.hse.gov.uk
www.osha.gov; 001 800 321 6742
www.craftscouncil.org.uk; +44 (0)207 806 2500

FINANCING YOUR BUSINESS
www.artscouncil.org.uk; +44 (0)845 300 6200
www.startupnation.com
www.businessfinanceforyou.co.uk
www.smallbusiness.co.uk
www.fundedbyme.com
www.fundingcircle.com
www.crowdcube.com
www.sba.gov; 001 800 827 5722

WRITING A BUSINESS PLAN
See contacts under Financing your business.
www.enterprisenation.com; +44 (0)1743 272555

MAKING CONNECTIONS
www.mentorsme.co.uk
www.nationalenterprisenetwork.org; +44 (0) 1234 831623
www.princes-trust.org.uk; +44 (0)800 842842
www.sba.gov, 001 800 827 5722

PROTECTING YOUR INTELLECTUAL PROPERTY
www.ipo.gov.uk; +44 (0)300 300 2000
www.icann.org
www.wipo.int; +41 22 338 8787
www.own-it.org
www.acid.uk.com; +44 (0)845 644 3617
www.uspto.gov; 001 800 786 9199
www.copyright.gov; 001 877 476 0778

USING SOCIAL MEDIA
www.blogger.com
www.livejournal.com
www.wordpress.com
www.twitter.com
www.facebook.com
www.pinterest.com

GETTING PROFESSIONAL PR HELP
In the UK, look for agencies that are members of the Chartered Institute
of Marketing (CIM) or the Chartered Institute of Public Relations (CIPR).
Members of both institutes work to a professional code of conduct.

ONLINE MARKETPLACES
www.ebay.co.uk
www.etsy.com
www.folksy.com
www.notonthehighstreet.com

OPENING YOUR OWN SHOP

www.appearhere.co.uk; +44 (0)203 021 0685
www.popupbritain.com
www.popupspace.com; +44 (0)1273 464 179
www.wearepopup.com; +44 (0)203 487 0813

MONEY, MONEY, MONEY...

www.cimaglobal.com; +44 (0)208 849 2251
www.icaew.com; +44 (0)1908 248 250
www.icas.org.uk; +44 (0)131 347 0100
www.cpadirectory.com
www.intuit.co.uk; +44 (0)808 168 9533
www.microsoft.com
www.pegasus.co.uk; + 44 (0)1536 495000
www.sage.co.uk; +44 (0)800 923 0344

TAX

www.hmrc.gov.uk
www.irs.gov; 001 800 829 4933

CARD AND ONLINE PAYMENTS

www.paypal.com/uk; +44 0800 358 7929
www.sagepay.com; +44 0845 322 4737

INSURANCE

Specialized insurance providers include:
Combined Market Traders Insurance Association www.cmtia.co.uk
G. M. Imbers and Sons www.gmimberltd.com; +44 (0)1342 327250
Public Art Online www.publicartonline.org.uk; +44 (0)121 7535301
Ian W. Wallace Ltd www.craftinsurance.co.uk; +44 (0)800 919359
You can also contact the British Insurance Broker's Association to find
an insurance broker near you: www.biba.org.uk/ConsumerHome.
aspx; +44 (0)870 950 1790

CUSTOMER LAW IN BRIEF

www.which.co.uk; +44 1992 822800
www.oft.gov.uk; +44 (0)8454 04 05 06
www.gov.uk/online-and-distance-selling-for-businesses
www.economie.gouv.fr/dgccrf

www.test.de
www.europa.eu

EMPLOYING STAFF
www.fca.org.uk; +44 (0)800 111 6768
www.hmrc.gov.uk
www.gov.uk/legal-right-to-work-in-the-uk
www.gov.uk/national-minimum-wage
Pay and Work Rights Helpline +44 (0)800 917 2368
www.dol.gov; 001 866 487 2365

Index

Credits

This book would not have been possible without the input of all our crafty contributors:

Hayley Banks, Emily Barnes, Claudia Boldt, Ruth Bonser, Donna Bramhall, Emily Dean, Jane Foster, Gillian Harris, Claire Hartley, Katie Hewett, Emma Jones, Sinead Koehler, Cat Morley, Daniel Phillips, Louise Presley, Sophie Simpson, Patricia van den Akker and Stephanie Weston Smith.

With special thanks to Clare Kelly and Sarah Hoggett for research, development and contributor interviews. And of course to the team at Mollie Makes, in particular Lara Watson, Helena Tracey and Katherine Raderecht.

Whatever the craft, we have the book for you – just head straight to Collins & Brown crafty HeadQuarters!

LoveCrafts is the one-stop destination for all things crafty, with the very latest news and information about all our books and authors. It doesn't stop there...

Enter our fabulous competitions and win great prizes
Download free patterns from our talented authors
Collect LoveCrafts loyalty points and receive
special offers on all our books

Join our crafting community at LoveCrafts –
we look forward to meeting you!